Perennials for Shade

Easy Plants for More Beautiful Gardens

Produced by Storey Communications, Inc.
Pownal, Vermont

Taylor's Guide is a registered trademark of Houghton Mifflin Company.

Library of Congress Cataloging-in-Publication Data

Perennials for shade : easy plants for more beautiful gardens.
        p.   cm. — (Taylor's 50 best)
     Includes index.
     ISBN 0-395-87331-2
     1. Perennials. 2. Shade-tolerant plants. I. Series.
  SB434.P4744 1999
  635.9'32 — dc21   98–44700

Printed in the United States of America

WCT 10 9 8 7 6 5 4 3 2 1

Perennials for Shade

Frances Tenenbaum, Series Editor

 HOUGHTON MIFFLIN COMPANY

Boston • New York   1999

CONTENTS

INTRODUCTION

Choosing perennials for a shade garden could be a daunting task, considering that most flowers need sun to bloom. Still, there are a surprising number of beautiful plants for part and even full shade. To help you make the selection, this guide lists the easiest-to-grow and best-performing perennials for these conditions. Each plant is shown in a full-color photo for easy identification. Included is information on where and how to grow the featured plant, along with horticultural tips and illustrations to assist you in making your shade-gardening adventure an enjoyable and educational endeavor.

What Is a Perennial for Shade?

Perennials are plants that persist year after year in a garden. They may be evergreen or deciduous, with the visible parts of the plants dying down each winter and new ones returning each spring from underground buds. Perennials that require part shade require an area that receives 3 to 4 hours of direct sun each day in the early morning or evening, but not at midday. Planting on the east or west side of a building provides this type of shade. Part shade is also the filtered light provided by shade trees that have had their lower limbs removed to provide direct sunlight for short periods as the sun shines through gaps in the foliage. Full shade is shade provided by the north side of a building or from the cover of dense evergreen trees. It takes a special plant to thrive in these conditions.

Soil Preparation

The key to successful gardening is adequate soil preparation. Unless you are blessed with good deep loam—soil that has been farmed, gardened, or worked to increase aeration, water-holding capacity, and organic matter—you will need to improve your garden soil by cultivation to raise its fertility level and increase its organic content. Soil for most perennials should be worked by turning it over with a shovel to a depth of 10 to 12 inches.

A fertile or rich soil is one where there is an ample supply of essential plant nutrients in a form that is readily available to plants.

Organic matter is vital to plants; it retains water in the soil and makes it available to plants, and it also provides food for bacteria that change nutrients into forms that can be absorbed by plants. Organic matter is decayed plant and animal remains; the best way to increase it is by adding some well-rotted compost (either purchased or homemade from garden debris or leaves), peat moss, or well-rotted horse or cow manure. (Poultry manure is usually too "hot" for most plants — i.e., it contains ammonia, which may burn the leaves or roots.) Seaweed is another excellent source of organic matter, but it is not readily available to all gardeners.

In soil that has a high sand or gravel content, many plants suffer from a lack of available water. The best way to increase the water-holding capacity of any soil is to increase its organic content. Conversely, wet soils need to be drained in order to increase the amount of oxygen that is available to plants. Soil drainage can be increased by adding organic matter (or very coarse sand, but organic matter is easier and supplies other benefits). Water should never stand over the crowns of most perennials for more than a few minutes after downpours—the exceptions are, of course, plants that naturally grow in wet spots. In very heavy clay soils, where making the soil hospitable to plants is tough, it is usually easier to build raised beds on top of the clay soil using bricks, fieldstone, pressure-treated lumber (except near edible plants), or naturally rot-resistant wood such as red cedar or locust as sides. Fill in the center with topsoil or compost.

Most perennials prefer soil that is slightly acidic (pH 6.5 to 6.8). To determine the pH of your soil, locate a soil-testing station in your area through the state Master Gardener's Program (home soil-testing kits are usually not very accurate). To adjust the pH, follow the recommendations of the soil-testing lab.

Fertilizing Plants

All plants need nutrients to maintain vigor. Some plants are heavy feeders and prefer frequent fertilizer applications; others are light feeders and only occasionally need supplementary feeding. Most perennials require a balanced fertilizer. The balance is between the three main ingredients—namely nitrogen (N), phosphorus (P), and potassium (K) — as well as trace elements such as iron, boron, copper, zinc, and magnesium. As a general rule, plants grown for their foliage require a high-nitrogen fertilizer, a formula in which the first number is largest, such as 10-5-5. Plants grown for their flowers usually benefit from a higher phosphorus content (a formula such as 5-10-5). Organic fertilizers generally release nutrients more slowly but last longer than standard synthetic fertilizers. Calcium, another essential mineral, is usually added in the form of limestone. This also raises the pH; in areas where the pH is already high, use agricultural gypsum.

Hardiness Zones

Each plant listed in this guide has a hardiness rating. Although these numbers represent the cold tolerance of the plants, the higher—or southern—number will indicate which plants will or will not survive the heat of the South. Refer to the map on page 121 to determine your hardiness zone.

Mulching and Winter Protection

Mulch is a 2- to 4-inch layer of organic matter laid on the soil surface to retain moisture in the soil and to keep down weed growth. Preferred mulch materials include pine needles, shredded bark, shredded leaves, and pine bark chips. Avoid peat moss, which forms a dry crust and prevents water from getting to the soil. Don't use fresh grass clippings, which heat up, or hay, which contains weed seeds. Mulch is best applied in fall as the plants are going dormant or in spring before they start to grow.

In cold climates, apply a 6- to 10-inch layer of winter protection around the crowns of plants after the ground is frozen in early winter, and remove it when forsythia blooms in spring. It is especially important after late-fall planting to prevent unestablished plants from heaving out of the soil during alternating mild and cold spells.

Planting Perennials

Perennials are sold in two ways—as bareroot and as container-grown plants. When planting a bareroot plant, dig a hole large enough so the roots can be spread out comfortably. Before planting, work a handful of a balanced fertilizer into the soil. Fill soil in around the roots and firm gently, making sure not to push down on the crown of the plant. Generally, the crown of the plant (where the stem meets the roots) should be just below soil level.

When planting pot- or container-grown plants, be sure to tease the roots apart. If this is not done, the roots may girdle each other and choke off their food and water supply. It is also important to set the plant in the soil at the same level as it was in the container.

Watering

Another key to successful gardening is watering. Provide too little water and plants perform poorly; too much and they're even worse. So how much is enough? First, all perennials should be well watered after planting. This settles the soil around the roots to establish good contact between the soil particles and newly developing root hairs. As a general rule, during the growing season most perennials require 1 inch of water per week. If it doesn't rain that amount, you will need to water them. Use a rain gauge situated in an open location to measure rain and irrigation. One sure way to "drown" perennials by overwatering is to put them on automatic timers that turn on irrigation water regardless of the amount of natural precipitation they receive.

How do you apply irrigation water? Perennials are best watered by soaker hoses; sprinklers have a tendency to weigh flowers down with water, splash mud on them, and encourage foliage diseases. A timer that turns the water on and off is a convenient way to use soaker hoses. Be sure not to overwater during naturally wet periods.

Controlling Pests and Diseases

Diagnosis is the key to pest and disease control. Ask for help from gardeners from the Master Gardening Programs found in most states, or try your local Cooperative Extension Service, or look for a book on garden pests to help identify and suggest preventative measures and possible cures. Use natural control methods wherever feasible; avoid broad-spectrum pesticides as much as possible—they are harmful to the user as well as the environment, and they kill good plants along with pests.

LADYBELLS
Adenophora confusa

Zones: 3–9

Bloom Time: Mid- to late summer

Light: Part shade

Height: 30–36 in.

Interest: Upright spikes of purple-blue flowers for weeks

This valuable bellflower relative from China is one of the few plants that bloom well in summer shade. Pretty spikes of purplish blue, bell-shaped blooms hang down like Chinese lanterns along the 30- to 36-inch vertical stems of ladybells. The bloom-laden spikes sit atop rich green foliage, flowering freely from mid- to late summer. This low-maintenance plant spreads but is not invasive and is long lived in areas with the right growing conditions. More heat tolerant than most of its relatives, this cheerful perennial fares well in the Southeast and much of the Southwest (except desert areas).

HOW TO GROW
Ladybells prefers deep, well-dug soil with good drainage and liberal amounts of organic matter worked in before planting. In early spring, mulch with 2 inches of leaf

compost around the crowns to maintain a moderately rich, evenly moist soil. Ladybells forms new plants by self-sowing, but it is noninvasive so it won't become a garden pest.

WHERE TO GROW

Equally happy in part shade and full sun, ladybells is suitable for a naturalized planting beside a shady walk under trees whose lower branches have been removed. It is also a good choice for more formal planting in a mixed border with perennials and shrubs. Since it is an excellent addition to floral arrangements, plant extra for cutting. Choose your location carefully, because the deep-growing, fleshy roots of ladybells resent being transplanted once established, and they usually outlive the gardener.

Top Choice

- *A. liliifolia,* lilyleaf ladybells, has fragrant, pale blue or creamy white, bell-shaped blossoms on 18- to 24-inch spikes. It is even more cold tolerant than common ladybells and is excellent for northern gardens. Zones 2 to 8.

Garden Companions

Ladybells adds a soft, subtle touch to shady gardens, complementing a wide range of plants from quiet and demure to bold and sassy, including:

- GLOBEFLOWER
- LADY FERN
- LADY'S-MANTLE
- MAIDENHAIR FERN
- MARGINAL SHIELD FERN
- ORIENTAL LILY
- RODGERSIA
- VARIEGATED LILYTURF

PLANTING UNDER TREES

Plant perennials under trees with deep roots such as oaks and white pines; they provide less competition for moisture and nutrients than do surface-rooting trees such as maples (especially Norway maples), beeches, and poplars. To allow more light to reach underplantings, remove the lower limbs of trees. (You can safely remove up to half the height of the tree.)

UPRIGHT BUGLE
Ajuga pyramidalis

Zones: 3–10

Bloom Time: Late spring

Light: Part shade

Height: 6–9 in.

Interest: Attractive ground cover with spikes of violet-blue flowers and a tidy, noninvasive habit

Upright bugle has showy 6- to 9-inch spikes of rich violet-blue blossoms and puts on quite a show when in bloom. After flowering, it makes a refined ground cover of dark green foliage. Unlike the more familiar common bugle that is widely used as a ground cover because it spreads like a weed, this cousin is a well-mannered, clump-forming plant. It is easy to grow and requires little maintenance once established.

HOW TO GROW

Although it prefers partial shade, upright bugle will tolerate sun if planted in rich, moist soil. It grows best in moist soil (never waterlogged) that is rich in organic matter. Before planting, incorporate lots of leaf compost or peat moss, especially if the soil is light and sandy. Mulching with 2 to 3 inches of leaf compost will keep soil moist and maintain a high humus level, a condition this plant favors. Keep plants looking neat by removing spent blossoms at the end of the bloom season. Plants can be divided easily almost any time, providing the soil is kept moist and the transplants are shaded from hot sun.

WHERE TO GROW

The most attractive plantings of upright bugle are those where large groups are situated in light shade under trees and large bushes. Upright bugle is ideal for a woodland garden, as well as on the east side of buildings, where it is shaded by the building during the brightest part of the day. Use it with other ground covers for a contrast in texture with a bonus of spring flowers.

Top Choices

- *A.* 'Metallica Crispa' has rich green foliage with a metallic gleam that sets off the purplish blue blossoms to best advantage.

- *A.* 'Metallica Crispa Purpurea' offers leaves of a dramatic reddish brown to purple hue.

- *A. genevensis,* Geneva bugle, another clump former, is smaller than upright bugle and has blue flowers. It is more drought tolerant than other bugles. 'Pink Beauty' has pink flowers. Zones 2 to 10.

- *A. reptans* 'Burgundy Glow' is a handsome blue-flowered variety of common bugle. Its gray-green leaves are variegated with pink and white. Be prepared to deal with its rambling habit.

CONTROLLING INVASIVE PLANTS

The best way to control invasive plants that spread with runners is to put down a barrier to block their path. In a bed, suitable blocking materials include logs and pressure-treated lumber. To stop common bugle from spreading into a lawn, use plastic lawn edging between the border and the lawn. Once bugle invades a lawn, the only reliable method of eradication is hand digging or using a broadleaf weed killer such as those used for dandelions.

SHADING TRANSPLANTS

Offer your transplants some extra shade protection to help preserve moisture and keep them stress-free. Shade cloth is ideal, especially over a large planting, but you can use all kinds of handy materials. Try poking a wooden shingle or board into the soil on the south side of each plant, or make a tepee out of plastic nursery flats or small pieces of plywood.

LADY'S-MANTLE
Alchemilla mollis

Zones: 3–9

Bloom Time: Summer

Light: Part shade

Height: 18–24 in.

Interest: Handsome, light green foliage and abundant, long-lasting clusters of greenish yellow flowers that blend with just about every color

In early summer, lady's-mantle covers itself with long-lasting chartreuse flowers, a unique shade in the plant world and one that complements almost every other garden hue. The starry blossoms make great cut flowers that remain attractive for two to three weeks. Its beautifully shaped large leaves are a pleasing light green and have the delightful habit of trapping jewel-like beads of water after rain or irrigation. The Latin name *Alchemilla* is derived from an association with ancient alchemists, who believed this plant had many medicinal properties.

HOW TO GROW
Lady's-mantle prefers part shade, but it can also be grown in full sun—providing the soil doesn't dry out in the heat of summer. It is happiest in soil that is rich in organic matter and holds moisture well but is also well

drained. Lady's-mantle requires little maintenance; the only chore is to remove the spent blossoms after they finally cease to delight the eye. In the Southeast, this plant sometimes succumbs to high humidity, so it is best to place it in areas where it has the necessary part shade and excellent air movement to keep it happy.

WHERE TO GROW

Lady's-mantle can be grown in woodland gardens, along a shady path, or as a foundation plant in front of evergreen bushes. Or try it in a mixed border, as a ground cover, or in a bed by itself. Lady's-mantle is a great neighbor for plants of almost any hue. Use it to complement flowers in cool colors such as blue, lavender, or white, or as a cool companion for hot yellow, orange, red, or purple hues. Cut flowers will never be missed from large plantings of lady's-mantle because it blooms profusely.

Top Choices

- *A. alpina,* alpine lady's-mantle, is a dwarf (6 to 8 inches) grown for its deeply lobed, dark green, silver-edged foliage. Its green flowers are not as showy as those of ordinary lady's-mantle. Zones 3 to 8.

- *A. erythropoda,* red-stemmed lady's-mantle, looks like a smaller version of lady's-mantle. Its lobed leaves are grayish and the flowers are less showy. Zones 4 to 9.

KEEPING PLANTS HEALTHY

Many shade-loving plants require rich, moist soil. An extended period of drought or even a week or two of hot, dry summer weather can damage even the hardiest plant. To keep your shade garden vigorous and healthy and unharmed during dry spells, try these easy methods:

1 At planting time be sure to mix compost or another type of organic matter into the soil. Organic matter helps the soil hold more water for longer periods of time.

2 After planting, and annually in spring and fall, add a layer of mulch around the base of the plants. Shredded bark, buckwheat or cocoa hulls, or aged wood chips are good choices. Mulches help block evaporation and keep the soil (and therefore plant roots) cooler, too.

3 Snake a soaker hose between the plants, then cover it with mulch. A soaker hose will put water right where it's needed. Just turn it on whenever the garden soil needs a soaking.

JAPANESE ANEMONE

Anemone x *hybrida*

Zones: 4–9

Bloom Time: Late summer and early fall

Light: Part shade

Height: 24–48 in.

Interest: Colorful blooms that are welcome in shade gardens when little else is blooming

Japanese anemone is the catchall name for a large group of late-summer- and fall-blooming hybrids. These heavy-blooming shade plants produce either single or double, pink or white blossoms that float like butterflies on wiry stems above clumps of maplelike foliage. For the late-season garden, Japanese anemones offer some of the brightest color spots. The yellow-centered, saucer-shaped blossoms are up to 3 inches across on many varieties and stand 3 to 5 feet tall; foliage clumps are about 2 feet high and wide.

HOW TO GROW

Set out hybrid anemones in spring or fall in a well-drained, slightly acidic, loamy soil in light shade or full sun. Before planting, incorporate a slow-release fertilizer into the soil along with generous portions of leaf mold, compost, or peat moss; adding a 1- to 2-inch layer of mulch helps preserve moisture. These perennials have little drought tolerance and will show browned foliage if moisture is lacking. During hot, dry summers, you may need to give them some extra water.

WHERE TO GROW

Lightly shaded sites are best for Japanese anemones. With some protection from sun, the plants grow robustly; they can even tolerate some neglect in regions where rainfall is plentiful. The more vigorous varieties spread by underground rhizomes to form colonies, a welcome addition to naturalized gardens. Plant small drifts of anemones in borders where the late-season foliage will cover holes left by spring bulbs or perennials that have died back. Fit them, also, into bays in shrub borders with azaleas or viburnums; in these locations, you may need to curb their spread.

Top Choices

- A. 'Honorine Jobert' has been a favorite for over a hundred years. Its snow white blossoms are highlighted by golden yellow centers. Flower stalks are 3 to 4 feet tall.

- A. 'Margarete' has semidouble flowers in a deep shade of raspberry-tinted pink.

- A. 'Prince Henry' has deep rose-pink, semidouble blossoms on 3-foot stems.

- A. 'Queen Charlotte' bears large, 3- to 4-inch, semidouble blossoms in clear pink on 3-foot stems.

WINTER PROTECTION

Mulching during the growing season provides many benefits for perennials (see page 73), but mulching for winter protection is a different kind of safeguard.

Many plants need winter protection to guard them against repeated thawing and freezing. Without insulation, shallow-rooted and freshly set plants are inevitably harmed when the movement of the soil heaves them out of the ground. Winter protection also prevents plants from drying out in cold winter winds.

❶ After the ground is well frozen, cover the entire plant with straw, salt-marsh hay, or pine needles.

❷ Add a layer of pine boughs or other available evergreen prunings; don't overlook the branches of a discarded Christmas tree.

❸ In spring, at about the time the forsythia blooms, remove the protective materials. You can shake off the pine needles or evergreen leaves and spread out the straw or hay to use as the first layer of spring mulch. Keep it away from the crowns of your plants where the new shoots are emerging.

SNOWDROP ANEMONE
Anemone sylvestris

Zones: 4–9

Bloom Time: Spring to early summer

Light: Part shade

Height: 12–18 in.

Interest: Solitary, nodding, snow white flowers that are slightly fragrant and bloom nonstop

Of the many and varied anemones, one of the most delightful is that spring charmer, the snowdrop anemone. Its small, cup-shaped flowers in pure white are dotted with tufts of yellow stamens in the centers. Each of the 2-inch blossoms stands alone atop wiry, 18-inch flower stalks that rise out of 12-inch mounds of divided blue-green leaves. This fast-growing perennial owes its strength to tough underground rhizomes that want to creep beyond the original planting and colonize shaded sites.

HOW TO GROW
Snowdrop anemone grows most vigorously in rich, light, and moist but well-drained soil. After bloom in summer, this species can tolerate some dryness; it also withstands more alkaline soils than do other anemones. If you cut the flower stems to the ground just after the blossoms

fade, snowdrop anemones are likely to reward you with a second bloom in fall. Stems left standing develop white, wooly seed heads.

WHERE TO GROW

This small sylvan native is perfect for naturalizing along the edges of deciduous woodlands. Its fast-growing nature has limited usefulness in a perennial garden, however, since it readily becomes too aggressive if conditions are ideal. You will appreciate snowdrop anemones most if you plant them where their runners can be contained or where they won't over-power more well-behaved perennials. In place of a lawn and where no traffic is allowed, this species makes a good ground cover among shrubs and low trees.

Top Choices

- A. 'Elsie Pleno' has double blossoms that are less refined than the common single blooms.

- A. 'Macrantha' is even more vigorous than the species. It produces large, abundant blossoms.

- A. *nemorosa*, European wood anemone, is another vigorous grower that flowers in spring and is easily naturalized in open woodlands. After its solitary white, pink, or lilac flowers fade, the foliage dies back.

PERENNIALS AS GROUND COVERS

Every ground cover should beautify the space it fills, protect the soil, and grow worry-free for years on end. Snowdrop anemones fulfill all the qualifications for a reliable ground cover:

- Snowdrop anemones shine in spring and early summer, when their dapper white blossoms dance above loose tussocks of foliage. Their beauty lasts through three seasons. They are most effective in climates where a covering of snow hides the bare ground or their browned foliage in winter.

- The fibrous underground stems and increasing numbers of compact new plants naturally spread out over woodland floors, covering the soil beneath. As long as they have shade and ample moisture, snowdrop anemones thrive in a wide range of soil conditions.

- Plant snowdrop anemones alone, without other perennials cluttering their space. Reserve this broad-leafed species for open woodlands where there is dappled sun flowing through high canopies; large shrubs lend a harmonious note as compatible companions. Little or no maintenance is required.

JACK-IN-THE-PULPIT

Arisaema triphyllum

Zones: 4–9

Bloom Time: Late spring to early summer

Light: Part to full shade

Height: 12–30 in.

Interest: Exotic flowers in shades of green and purple; brilliant scarlet fruit clusters follow

Jack-in-the-pulpit is widespread in the woods of the eastern United States. Heights and colors vary, even in the same area. "Jack" (the reproductive organs, also called the spadix, of this fanciful plant) stands in a "pulpit" (a cuplike structure that is covered by a spathe, a colorful bract that arches over). The unusual blossoms remain attractive for several weeks before the fruits (mature Jacks) swell to a bright emerald green, then turn to scarlet red. Although not poisonous, the fruits cause a severe irritation to the mouth. Since the fruits look like candy, take care to keep small children away. Native Americans used the tubers to make a starchy food by boiling out the irritant and grinding and drying the mash into a type of flour.

HOW TO GROW

Jack-in-the-pulpit is anything but fussy and requires no maintenance. To keep it happy, plant in humus-rich soil that retains moisture without staying soggy. Jack-in-the-pulpit can be planted or transplanted at any time of the year when the soil is workable—just add lots of organic matter (leaf compost or peat moss) before planting. To form new colonies, transplant the seedlings that spring up around the parent plants.

WHERE TO GROW

Jack-in-the-pulpit is a wildflower that belongs in woodland or shady gardens, where it will put on an unusual show. Since it will tolerate heavy shade, try it on the north side of buildings and under evergreen trees. It looks really striking planted amid low-growing ferns that will hide the bare spot left when the Jack goes dormant in midsummer. This plant seeds itself to form a colony, but it will never become an invasive pest.

Top Choices

- *A. sikokianum*, Japanese Jack-in-the-pulpit, is perhaps the most beautiful species with its purple-and-white, upward-pointing spathes on 18- to 24-inch plants. Zones 5 to 8.

- *A. speciosum*, showy cobra lily, is striped dark maroon-brown and white with huge leaves. It grows 24 to 36 inches tall. Zones 6 to 9.

WILDFLOWERS FROM SEEDS

Many woodland wildflowers can be increased by collecting the seeds and sowing them in a bed of humus-rich soil in a bright location similar to where you find them, or sow them in a spot that receives only early-morning or evening sun.

1 Scatter the seeds thinly, then cover with a thin layer of pine needles and water gently.

2 Transplant the seedlings the following spring as soon as they are large enough to handle. Some wildflowers need to grow for a couple of years before they are ready to bloom.

3 Jack-in-the-pulpit grows easily from seeds; collect the red berries in early fall, remove the pulp around the seeds, and plant them right away.

ITALIAN ARUM
Arum italicum 'Marmoratum'

Zones: 6–10

Bloom Time: Spring

Light: Part shade

Height: 12–18 in.

Interest: Showy white flowers; bright orange-red fruits; highly ornamental foliage

Italian arum, the Eurasian counterpart of Jack-in-the-pulpit, has a showy white spathe that lasts for several weeks in spring. Its flower looks like a miniature calla lily. The unusual blossom is followed by a cluster of bright green fruits that ripen to a striking orange-red. The arrowhead-shaped foliage doesn't appear until late summer and remains green over winter, disappearing in summer. Like Jack-in-the-pulpit, Italian arum contains an irritant (nonpoisonous); eating it is unpleasant and inadvisable.

HOW TO GROW

If you give it the conditions it likes, Italian arum will reward you with no effort on your part (other than replacing mulch every year or so). Plant it in humus-rich soil that retains moisture but doesn't stay wet in summer when the plant is dormant. This plant tolerates dry summers but needs ample moisture the rest of the year (whenever shoots or leaves are visible).

WHERE TO GROW

Italian arum belongs in woodland and shady wildflower gardens. In mild climates its foliage is superb for adding winter interest to the garden. In northern climates it can be grown in a sheltered location near the foundation if protected from icy winter blasts. It is a highly ornamental plant for all seasons except summer. Italian arum is an excellent container plant when grown in a cool greenhouse or conservatory.

Top Choices

- *A.* 'Pictum' is very similar to 'Marmoratum', but its leaves are decorated with creamy white markings.

- *A. maculatum*, lords-and-ladies or cuckoopint, is graced with creamy yellow spathes and spotted, shiny, green leaves. Its fruits ripen to orange-red clusters on 12- to 15-inch stalks.

Garden Companions

Italian arum goes well with plants that exhibit rich foliage or bear pleasing blossoms, such as:

- ADONIS
- CHRISTMAS FERN
- CHRISTMAS ROSE
- CORALBELLS
- HEARTLEAF BERGENIA
- SNOWDROP
- SPECIES CROCUSES
- WINTER ACONITE

UNIQUE "FLOWERS"

The "flowers" of Italian arum (also Jack-in-the-pulpit and calla lily) are made up of two parts. The largest is a modified leaf or bract that is often showy and is called a spathe. The second part is the flower spike or spadix that forms the "Jack" in Jack-in-the-pulpit. The reproductive organs are located on the spadix, which often ripens into a spike of colorful berries to provide garden interest after the flowers fade.

GOATSBEARD
Aruncus dioicus

Zones: 4–9

Bloom Time: Early summer

Light: Part shade

Height: 4–6 ft.

Interest: Attractive, pale green, fernlike foliage and spectacular plumes of creamy white flowers

Goatsbeard has been warmly welcomed into many shady gardens because of its huge, feathery plumes of creamy white flowers. Like its relative astilbe (see pages 28 to 31), it is equally happy in full sun, but only where summers are not too hot and the soil is consistently moist throughout the growing season. In its native habitat, goatsbeard even grows in wet, marshy areas, so it is almost impossible to overwater it in your garden. Like its stubborn namesake, the mature plant requires a backhoe or dynamite to force it out of the ground; it is best left where first established.

HOW TO GROW

For goatsbeard to thrive, it requires humus-rich soil that doesn't dry out in summer. Be sure to enhance the soil with lots of organic matter at planting time and make sure that the soil is well moistened before adding mulch to hold in moisture. Water well during summer dry spells. Staking isn't necessary except in areas that get hit with frequent torrential downpours when the plant is in bloom. Maintenance is easy—remove spent blossoms and cut down the plant when it dies back in late fall.

WHERE TO GROW

Goatsbeard is a large plant that requires lots of room. This elegant plant will grace any property that has high shade in the afternoon—under tall trees, at the north side of a tall shrub, or in a woodland garden. Its stately presence is wonderful in the back of a border where, as it matures, it will dominate its neighbors for several weeks. It sets off other tall plants such as delphiniums (don't keep the soil wet around these plants, though!) and provides a foil for herbaceous peonies, the real show-offs of the plant world. For a more subtle and refined combination, plant Siberian iris in front of goatsbeard.

Top Choices

- *A.* 'Kneiffii' is a smaller version with even more attractive, lacier foliage on a 36-inch plant.

- *A. aethusifolius* is a dainty miniature goatsbeard (from Korea) with white flowers and very lacy foliage on an 8- to 12-inch plant. It belongs at the front edge of any woodland garden and beside every shady path.

PROPAGATING BY DIVISION

You can create a new plant with vegetative propagation—either rooting a piece or dividing the entire plant into several pieces. The new plants will be identical to the parent from which they were obtained. To divide a plant:

1 Carefully dig up the entire plant when it is dormant—in either very early spring or midfall.

2 Carefully shake off excess soil to expose the crown, where roots meet the top of the plant.

3 Examine the crown to determine where dormant buds are located and which pieces can be separated that will include dormant buds.

4 Gently pull plants apart to divide them, or use pruners or a sharp knife to separate the pieces. For really tough plants, such as daylilies and ornamental grasses, force two garden forks placed back to back into the middle of the plant to force the clump apart.

EUROPEAN WILD GINGER
Asarum europaeum

Zones: 4–8

Bloom Time:
Inconspicuous flowers

Light: Part to full
shade

Height: 6 in.

Interest: Heart-shaped,
shiny, dark green
leaves that make a
very desirable mat-
forming evergreen
ground cover

European wild ginger is an easy-care, spreading foliage plant that looks good all season long. It spreads in a noninvasive manner, making it an ideal ground cover for areas with part or full shade. The flowers are a nondescript greenish brown. Tucked under the foliage, they play no role in the ornamental value of this evergreen plant. The roots smell of ginger when bruised or cut—hence the common name. Clusters of the shiny, round leaves make a perfect backdrop for a nosegay of violets or a bouquet of other tiny flowers.

HOW TO GROW
Shade is a must—either light or fairly heavy. (See page 109 for an explanation of different types of shade.) As with many shade lovers, rich, moist, but well-drained soil that doesn't dry out in summer is also essential. Work

lots of leaf compost or peat moss into the soil before planting, then mulch with a thin layer of leaf compost in late fall or late winter. Water well during dry spells in summer. Unlike some ground covers, there is no need to remove the spent flowers of European wild ginger to maintain its attractiveness. In addition, the leaf cover is enough to suppress most weeds. Seedlings often appear under large clumps; transplant them as soon as they are large enough to handle.

WHERE TO GROW

Wild ginger is a valuable ground cover to plant alongside woodland paths and at the front of woodland gardens. The elegant foliage is equally at home in more formal and shady urban settings. To create an exciting interplay of textures, place it alongside low-growing ferns, dwarf astilbes, and dwarf hostas. It is especially pleasing when underplanted with small spring-flowering bulbs such as crocus or Siberian squill.

Top Choices

- *A. canadense,* Canadian ginger, is native to eastern woodlands and blessed with downy, deciduous, 3-inch leaves on a spreading plant with insignificant flowers. Zones 4 to 9.

- *A. shuttleworthii,* shuttleworth ginger, is another native worth seeking out for its very attractive, mottled, evergreen foliage. 'Callaway' is an even showier selection. Both are better in heat than other wild gingers. Zones 5 to 9.

WOODLAND PLANTING

On walks through the woods, it is always magical to encounter a place that seems like a natural garden. It could be as simple as a spray of wildflowers growing amid a cluster of boulders, or a winding path lined with ferns. Here are some easy tips for creating your own woodland planting:

1 Locate your woodland planting beneath a canopy of trees. Deciduous or mixed deciduous and evergreen trees provide the best setting.

2 Forests often have a rich but shallow top layer of humus-rich soil with a deep layer of mineral-rich soil beneath. When planting in this type of soil, dig a hole twice as large as is needed and improve the removed soil with lots of compost. This creates fertile pockets of rich soil that will help plants establish more quickly.

3 Choose native plants that thrive in the habitat that naturally occurs in local woodlands. Other good choices include plants that have become naturalized in your area.

4 Plan a path through the planted area and be sure to stay on it. Woodland plantings are often more fragile than other types of gardens.

HYBRID ASTILBE
Astilbe x *arendsii*

Zones: 4–9

Bloom Time: Summer

Light: Part shade

Height: 22–48 in.

Interest: Plumes of flowers in many shades of pink, red, or white; one of the most rugged garden plants

Astilbe puts on the most spectacular show of any shade-loving plant. When in bloom, 12- to 24-inch-long, many-branched flower spikes shine brilliantly in lavender to rose-pink, in blood red to salmon and magenta, and in creamy, rosy, and snowy white. The lacy, fernlike foliage grows in clumps 2 to 4 feet high and nearly as wide. It remains attractive from its first appearance in spring until it is covered by winter frost or snow. Some selections have stunning bronze leaves. Most of the garden astilbes are the Arends hybrids.

HOW TO GROW
Astilbe requires humus-rich soil that retains moisture yet is fast draining. Some varieties are more drought tolerant than others, but all must have adequate moisture in either sun or shade or their foliage will shrivel and

brown. Avoid planting astilbe in boggy conditions; it will succumb to rot in too much water, especially while dormant in winter. Incorporate ample amounts of well-decomposed compost, aged manure, peat moss, or leaf mold into the soil before planting. After planting, add a 2- to 3-inch layer of mulch—pine needles or shredded bark—over the surface to hold in moisture. The browned flower spikes remain attractive in autumn, but your astilbes will look tidier and bloom more heavily the next year if you trim off the dried flower stalks.

WHERE TO GROW

Hybrid astilbe belongs in every border with moist soil. Its glossy foliage adds refinement to any planting all season long. Enjoy months of color by selecting those with early, midseason, and late bloom periods. When introducing astilbes into a woodland habitat, choose varieties with a loose, arching habit; reserve the stiffly upright growers for more formal locations in borders or along foundations.

Top Choices

- A. 'Bressingham Beauty' grows to 3 feet tall with bronze-tinted foliage; its flowers are bright pink and slightly drooping.

- A. 'Fanal' is one of the most popular of all astilbes. Its deep, bloodred, narrow floral spikes open in late spring. The leaves are dark bronze-green.

- A. 'Irrlicht' begins blooming in spring. Its pale pink flowers fade to white in a spectacular show over dark green foliage. Clumps are about 30 inches tall.

OTHER ASTILBES

A. *chinensis* 'Pumila' is a 10- to 12-inch dwarf whose lovely pink spikes are flushed with lilac. This robust variety grows so vigorously that it needs frequent division. It's one of the most heat and drought tolerant of all astilbes and makes an excellent ground cover. Varieties of this species vary considerably in height. Among those that are commonly 20 inches tall are bright pink 'Finale', salmon pink 'Intermezzo', and reddish pink 'Serenade'.

A. *c.* var. *taguetii* 'Purple Lance' has stiffly erect, 36- to 48-inch, purplish red spikes that add a striking vertical accent to the border in midsummer. 'Superba' is similar, lavender-purple, and somewhat shorter.

COMPANION BULBS

Spring-blooming bulbs are ideal companions for early-blooming astilbes; the grasslike bulb foliage contrasts nicely with young, ferny astilbe leaves. Plant groups of fritillarias, lilies, and snowdrops (*Galanthus* spp.) for color interest in beds and borders as the astilbes leaf out and begin their bloom.

DWARF ASTILBE
Astilbe simplicifolia

Zones: 4–9

Bloom Time: Summer

Light: Part shade

Height: 12–18 in.

Interest: plumes of flowers in many shades of pink, red, or white; one of the most rugged garden plants

This group of dwarf astilbes is sometimes called the star astilbes for the starlike blossoms that grace their dense, pyramidal flower plumes. The leafy clumps attain a height of little more than 1 foot, have small individual leaves, and are somewhat slower growing than other species; the foliage of some varieties is tinted bronze or burgundy. If you're tempted to cut the plumy flowers for indoor arrangements, you'll be happy with them only briefly, for their blossoms quickly fade. After bloom in the garden, the browned seed heads continue to decorate plants. You can leave them standing throughout winter or you can cut them back after the first hard frost. Astilbes are most effective when massed in groups of five or more to create swaths of color running through your garden beds.

HOW TO GROW

Check the soil moisture throughout summer wherever you plant your astilbes. Their shallow roots are easily damaged by dry conditions and you may need to irrigate if summer rains are scarce. All species like their roots shaded with mulch and their top growth in shade for several hours during midday unless you live in a cool, coastal area where the soil stays constantly moist.

WHERE TO GROW

These low-growing astilbes are wonderfully versatile in the garden. Plant them in combination with other perennials and ferns in low borders or use them as accents alongside a garden bench, under small trees, or in a rock garden. You can create spectacular effects by alternating with taller plants. If you introduce astilbes into a woodland scene, choose varieties with a loose, arching habit; reserve the stiffly upright growers for more formal locations in borders or along foundations.

Top Choices

- A. 'Aphrodite' forms compact, 12- 14-inch clumps; blossoms are carmine to salmon red.

- A. 'Atrorosea' grows to nearly 2 feet and produces arching floral sprays in salmon pink.

- A. 'Bronze Elegans' has rose-pink flowers in late summer framed by dark, glossy, bronze foliage.

- A. 'Sprite' is one of the most popular. Its 12-inch-tall foliage is bronze toned and its arching plumes are shell pink.

COORDINATING STRONG COLORS

Achieving color harmony in your garden can be hit or miss, especially when working with strong tones and unfamiliar plants. Rather than having to remove blossoms that clash offensively after they bloom in the "wrong" spot, test them first.

- Try to see a plant in bloom before you purchase it. Photos aren't always reliable; many colors are easily distorted on film.

- Rather than planting an unfamiliar perennial in a permanent location, grow it temporarily in a nursery bed until it blooms. In the meantime, fill in holes in your garden with seasonal annuals. Once the test plants are in bloom, set flower sprays in vases where you'd like your plant to grow permanently and evaluate the color compatibility with its associates.

- Astilbes are one perennial that you'll want to plant carefully to avoid garish pairings. Many varieties are intensely hued and will clash sharply with neighbors of similar colors. These must be widely separated or framed by quiet creamy pastels or solid greens. Wherever you place astilbes, be sure to mass them; groups of five or more of same color create the best effect.

HEARTLEAF BERGENIA

Bergenia cordifolia

Zones: 3–9

Bloom Time: Spring

Light: Part shade

Height: 18 in.

Interest: Attractive clusters of pink, white, or red flowers above handsome, glossy evergreen foliage that turns red in fall

Heartleaf bergenia is one of the best-kept secrets of shade gardening. Native to regions of central Asia, this hardy plant has thick, shiny leaves that remain green through winter, even in cold northern areas. In spring, nodding clusters of pink, white, or rosy red flowers rise on succulent stalks to peek above the mantle of leaves. As useful and beautiful as heartleaf bergenia is, it has been overlooked by many gardeners until recently. Increased availability and new varieties with richly colored flowers and foliage promise to make this plant a popular choice for shade gardens.

HOW TO GROW

Heartleaf bergenia adapts to a wide range of conditions. It grows best in moist, slightly acidic soil that is rich in organic matter. In cool regions in moist soil, it can grow in full sun, but the foliage looks best under the filtered light of high trees. In the South, grow heartleaf bergenia in part to full shade. In cold regions with unreliable snow cover, protect plants in winter with a thick layer of straw or salt hay added in late fall.

WHERE TO GROW

Heartleaf bergenia can be used in the same manner as hosta (pages 60 to 63). Plant as an edging along walkways or to define the front of the perennial border. It makes an excellent ground cover under deciduous trees and is a good accent plant for shady rock or water gardens. Heartleaf bergenia is especially nice in clumps along a woodland trail in the company of primroses and ferns.

Top Choices

- *B.* 'Bressingham White' has 15-inch-tall flower stalks covered with pink buds that open to white blossoms above a mantle of dark evergreen foliage.

- *B.* 'Bressingham Ruby' is similar to 'Bressingham White' but has red flowers and deeper fall color.

- *B.* 'Rotblum' ('Red Bloom') has ruby red flowers on 16-inch-tall flower stalks above evergreen leaves.

- *B.* 'Perfect' has very large evergreen leaves and nodding pink flower clusters.

GARDEN HUMOR

"Pig squeak" is another name for heartleaf bergenia. This novel epithet was earned in the misty past when someone stumbled on an odd coincidence between bergenia and pigs.

The thick green leaves of bergenia have a glossy, somewhat sticky coating. When conditions are just right, the leaves (with a little help from you) can be urged to emit a strange little sound reminiscent of a pig's squeak. Learning to make bergenia squeak doesn't make you a better gardener, but does make garden parties and backyard barbecues more entertaining.

To make heartleaf bergenia squeak:

❶ Sprinkle water over the leaves.

❷ Wet your forefinger and thumb. Grasp the top of the leaf with your thumb and the bottom with your forefinger.

❸ Firmly but gently rub your fingers together. They should initially slide across the leaf, then gradually become almost sticky. It is then that the characteristic squeak makes itself heard.

SIBERIAN BUGLOSS
Brunnera macrophylla

Zones: 3–10

Bloom Time: Spring

Light: Part shade

Height: 12–18 in.

Interest: Tiny blue flowers over heart-shaped leaves

This rugged perennial has tiny, brilliant sky blue flowers like forget-me-nots (unrelated) that twinkle against its large, dark green, heart-shaped foliage. When in bloom, Siberian bugloss is stunning; for the remainder of the season, its foliage adds texture and an interesting leaf shape to any shade garden. This tough, low-maintenance plant makes a fine ground cover.

HOW TO GROW

Siberian bugloss requires well-drained soil that is rich in organic matter to help it retain moisture. Plants will tolerate morning sun in moist sites and need more shade in drier sites. Mulch well and water plants thoroughly during summer dry spells. Slugs can be a problem (see "Removing Slugs" at right), but apart from dealing with this pest, Siberian bugloss requires no other maintenance.

WHERE TO GROW

Rugged Siberian bugloss is at home at the edge of a woodland garden as well as along a shady path where its charm can be easily enjoyed. It looks superb planted with late-flowering narcissus (especially jonquil), because they flower at similar times. Underplant it with true lilies to provide summer color. This lovely perennial makes an interesting ground cover under small-growing shrubs such as deciduous azalea, red-stemmed dogwood, and sweet pepperbush.

Top Choices

- *B.* 'Langtree' is a variegated form that requires cool shade to look good; its leaves are speckled with attractive aluminum spots.

- *B.* 'Variegata' is a stunning, 14-inch plant with creamy white leaf edges; it requires a cool, shady location, because leaves will scorch in hot sun.

REMOVING SLUGS

Slugs can't be eliminated, for they are ever-present in moist spots, but their impact on ornamental plants can be reduced. Protect pets and wildlife by avoiding poison slug baits. Sprays are also ineffective, because they wash away in the rain or while plants are being watered. Try slug barriers (see page 89) or one or more of the following methods of removal:

- Pick slugs off at night when they feed. Locate them with a flashlight and use rubber gloves for slugs so they don't "slime" you. (If you get slime on your skin, remove with rubbing alcohol.)

- Trap slugs by placing grapefruit halves upside down throughout the garden (first eat the fruit and scrape out any remaining membranes). Check traps in the morning; dispose of any containing slugs.

- The classic way to trap slugs is with beer. Sink shallow dishes such as margarine tubs into the soil so the rim is level with the ground. Fill three-quarters full with beer. Empty when the "trap" contains several slugs, rinse, and reuse.

FAIRY CANDLES
Cimicifuga racemosa

Zones: 3–9

Bloom Time: Mid- to late summer

Light: Part shade

Height: 6–8 ft.

Interest: Candles of long, elegant, white flower spikes that tower above foliage

In most catalogs and garden books, this plant is usually called black cohosh, black snakeroot, or bugbane—totally unflattering names for a highly desirable plant. Fairy candles (the name used by Dr. Edgar Wherry, a noted native plant botanist) is so much more appropriate and descriptive! This graceful eastern American native has found a home in woodlands and large borders around the world. When in flower it dominates any planting with its tall fairy wands of white blossoms. This large plant requires space, so plant it where it can spread, such as in a bed of hostas or ferns.

HOW TO GROW
Fairy candles must have rich, moist soil that drains well. In dry locations the leaves turn brown and may drop off, so mulch well and water heavily during dry spells.

Staking isn't usually necessary, but over-feeding with plant food may cause the stems to grow so luxuriantly that they lean after a period of high winds. As a precaution in windy locations, place tall, very thin bamboo canes around the plant and tie green string loosely to "corset" the stems. No other care is needed, except to remove the spent blossoms and feed with compost or aged manure every year or two. In a "wild" situation, allow the spent flower spikes to go to seed and they will self-sow to produce even more of this delightful plant.

WHERE TO GROW

Fairy candles is at home in the center of a large island bed; at the back of a one-sided border; in a wild, woodland garden where it can spread freely; and as a tall feature in a bed of a ground cover such as pachysandra, periwinkle, ivy, or hosta. It likes part shade but will grow in full sun if ample moisture is provided. It isn't particularly fond of the heat and humidity of the Deep South.

Top Choices

- *C. racemosa* 'Atropurpurea' is a stunning "black-leafed" (actually dark purple) selection with contrasting white flowers on 4- to 6-foot stems in summer.

- *C. simplex* 'White Pearl' has white spikes on 36- to 48-inch plants in late fall and is good for a mass planting.

Garden Companions

Fairy candles is a bold plant that can overpower some of the more subtle shade plants. For best effect, plant fairy candles with large-leafed ferns and graceful but assertive-looking perennials such as the ones below:

- BIGLEAF GOLDENRAY
- GREAT SOLOMON'S-SEAL
- HOSTA (LARGE-LEAFED)
- JAPANESE ANEMONE
- LEMON LILY
- MAIDEN GRASS
- UMBRELLA PLANT

FADED
FLOWERS

Most garden flowers lose their appeal and become ratty looking as color fades and petals shrivel. The tidy gardener never waits for them to brown completely, but deadheads spent flowers regularly, to stimulate a repeat bloom. Some perennials, such as fairy candles, continue to decorate the garden as their blossoms dry. You can leave the dried bottlebrush blooms standing on the tall stems of fairy candles until you cut the dead foliage back in late fall.

LILY-OF-THE-VALLEY
Convallaria majalis

Zones: 2–8

Bloom Time: Mid- to late spring

Light: Part shade

Height: 6–8 in.

Interest: Pure white bells of exquisitely fragrant flowers; handsome green foliage

No garden is complete without a bed of lily-of-the-valley to cut for the kitchen windowsill or bedside table. Many gardeners consider it indispensable for its uniquely fragrant flowers and broad, smooth, green leaves of a very pleasant hue. In cool-climate gardens, it is a pleasingly invasive plant that likes to romp in the woods; it will spread until it reaches either a tree, rock, log, water, or other barrier. Once planted, it is hard to eliminate and will generally outlive the one who planted it by a century or two. To ensure blooms the first year (for a daughter's wedding, for example), make sure you buy pips (the underground stem with a dormant flower bud at the end) guaranteed to bloom the first year. Small nonflowering pips are often sold; these take a year or two to produce blooms.

HOW TO GROW

Lily-of-the-valley is undemanding and tolerates almost any soil. For the best results, provide humus-rich soil and keep the plants well watered (not soggy) during the growing season. They are maintenance-free except for an occasional mulch with leaf compost or well-rotted manure in areas where the soil is lean.

WHERE TO GROW

Choose a location with care so your ancestors won't curse you for planting lily-of-the-valley "in the wrong place" because it has taken over in the garden. Plant it under shade trees and provide a barrier such as lawn edging to prevent invasive spreading.

Lily-of-the-valley is also a good seasonal indoor plant—even easier to force than spring bulbs. Special forcing varieties with extra-large pips are available to force in winter, providing delightful spring fragrance in a midwinter room. Transplant to the garden after danger of frost has passed.

Top Choices

- C. 'Fortin's Giant' towers (by lily-of-the-valley standards) to 12 to 15 inches and has large flowers. It is the best variety for forcing indoors.

- C. 'Prolificans' (also sold as 'Flora Plena') is a double-flowered selection that stays in bloom longer than the species. Plants spread more slowly.

- C. 'Rosea' is a lovely pink-flowered variety that looks good on its own or mingled into a stand of the ordinary white-flowered type.

FORCING
LILY-OF-THE-VALLEY

The pips for forcing often come in bundles of a dozen or two. To force bloom, follow these easy steps:

1 Use a bowl or pot that has a drainage hole to prevent the soil from becoming waterlogged. Add ordinary houseplant potting soil to within a couple of inches of the rim.

2 Determine which end of each pip has the flower bud and trim the other end to a length of 4 inches.

3 Place as many pips as can fit in the pot so that they are spaced 1 to 1½ inches apart in the soil. Add potting soil to cover.

4 Place the pot in a dark, warm place until the buds start to grow (usually about three to four days). Then move to a cool room with bright light but not direct sun. Blossoms should develop in about twenty-one days.

5 After blossoming, keep the plants in a cool room and water as they dry out. Plant outside in spring.

Yellow Corydalis
Corydalis lutea

Zones: 5–9

Bloom Time: Spring and summer

Light: Part shade

Height: 12–15 in.

Interest: Grayish green, fernlike foliage with masses of golden yellow flowers from late spring to late summer

It's definitely worth getting down on your knees for a closer look at yellow corydalis. This charming plant has exquisite golden yellow flowers that bear a close resemblance to their kin, the bleeding-heart. The blossoms are set off by lacy, fernlike, grayish green leaves that add even more visual appeal. Since it has a proclivity for spreading freely with self-sown seedlings, yellow corydalis will happily form a colony as large as you allow. It shows up in paths, rock walls—even in chunks of dirt in your garden cart if you're not too faithful about emptying it. Call it weedy if you dare; a plant is only a weed if it grows in the wrong place—so just accept this delightful plant wherever it appears. If you insist on keeping it in bounds, look for clusters of bluish green seedlings in spring and hoe them down on a bright sunny morning.

HOW TO GROW

Plant yellow corydalis in moist, woodsy soil. Water it, then forget it—until it flowers, of course. Maintenance? Nil. If you have an unusually dry summer, it will appreciate an occasional drink. Propagate from seeds—but instead of collecting the seeds and sowing them, just look around the parent plant for the bluish green seedlings that appear in spring. Transplant them to garden spots where you want long-lasting color, or give them to a friend whose garden needs a boost.

WHERE TO GROW

Plant yellow corydalis along a woodland path or anywhere in a woodland garden where it can frolic freely. While it tolerates full sun in cool, moist climates, it does best in some shade. It doesn't handle desert climates or extreme heat well.

Top Choices

- C. *cheilanthifolia,* ferny corydalis, has showy yellow flowers and beautiful fronds of lacy foliage on 9- to 12-inch plants. A more refined form than the yellow corydalis, it is also less rambunctious about spreading in most gardens.

- C. 'Blue Panda', blue corydalis, is a recent introduction that has taken the gardening world by storm with its incredible blue flowers and lacy foliage on 12- to 15-inch plants. It may go dormant where summers are hot and dry.

Garden Companions

Yellow corydalis blends with any blue- yellow- or gold-flowering plant from early spring through summer. Plant it for color under the light shade of ferns or evergreen shrubs.

- BLUE-EYED MARY
- CORALBELLS
- CREEPING PHLOX
- EPIMEDIUM
- LENTEN ROSE
- PRIMROSE
- SIBERIAN BUGLOSS
- TUFTED VIOLET
- WILD BLUE PHLOX

A DRY STONE WALL

The most delectable location for yellow corydalis is at the top of a dry stone wall, where you can examine its charming flowers more closely without stooping. It will scatter its seeds until the whole wall becomes a mass of sparkling yellow blooms; to encourage this further, spread a little humus-rich soil in the crevices. You don't have a stone wall? It's worth building one for yellow corydalis!

MAIDEN PINK
Dianthus deltoides

Zones: 4–7

Bloom Time: Late spring and summer

Light: Part shade

Height: 6–12 in.

Interest: Masses of vivid, cheery flowers over mats of bright green, grassy foliage

The maiden pink is a delightful carpet-forming plant from Europe that throws an abundance of twinkling, slightly fragrant blossoms over wiry 6- to 12-inch stems. They appear in brilliant shades of crimson, rose, scarlet, or purplish red; there are also pure white selections, some with a crimson eye ring. This, along with sweet William, is the only pink that will tolerate shade; it provides late-spring and early-summer color.

HOW TO GROW
Maiden pink is happy in part shade, bright indirect light, or full sun. It requires organic, rich garden soil that is well drained and near neutral to slightly alkaline (work dolomitic limestone into acidic soil before planting). After blossoming is over, be sure to shear the plants down to the foliage to encourage a second flush of blooms.

WHERE TO GROW

Maiden pink makes an excellent edging plant for borders, herb gardens, and lightly shaded woodland paths. It also serves well as a ground cover under and beside small shrubs or on a bank, and it's a lovely sight cascading from the top of a stone wall. If the stone wall puts it within easy reach of your nose so you can appreciate its delicate fragrance, so much the better. It does not thrive in the hot, humid summers of the Deep South.

Top Choices

- D. 'Albus' produces masses of flowers in purest white, especially lovely when illuminated by lamplight or moonlight.

- D. 'Zing Rose' is one of the most widely available maiden pinks, with deep rose-red flowers decorated with a dainty, darker center ring. Plants grow to 6 inches tall.

- D. *barbatus*, sweet William, is the only other member of the dianthus clan that tolerates some shade. It produces rich green foliage and flat-topped clusters of flowers on 10- to 18-inch stems. An ancient favorite of cottage gardeners, its flower colors include shades of pink, red, and white. Some of the showiest are a combination of colors, and some have a slight fragrance. Plant from seeds or nursery starts. Sweet William acts like a biennial in northern climates (a true perennial in the South), but since it often self-sows, it will keep coming back.

SHEARING FOR NEW BLOOMS

Many perennials benefit from an early-summer shearing as their flowers fade. Trimming off browned blossoms gives plants a well-groomed look, but it also has the benefit of promoting new growth and more abundant repeat blooms. Before you begin trimming back any plant, however, look at its growth habit to see what kind of cuts you should make and how drastically you need to trim the flowering stems.

- Plants like maiden pink that grow in neat mats need to have all of the flowering stalks cut back to the top of the low-growing foliage. New stems will rise and produce flowers at their tips.

- Cut individual stems to the ground on flowering clumps such as coralbells, lilyturf, and primroses.

- On taller plants that produce multiple stems in clumps, such as foxglove or ladybells, cut flowering stalks back about one-third to where new growth shows above an older leaf.

BLEEDING-HEART
Dicentra x 'Luxuriant'

Zones: 3–9

Bloom Time: Summer

Light: Part to deep shade

Height: 15 in.

Interest: Reddish pink, heart-shaped blooms over lacy, fernlike foliage all season long

As its name implies, 'Luxuriant' bleeding-heart has heart-shaped blossoms, split at the bottom to show their paler inner petals. This shade-loving perennial is a hybrid of East and West Coast natives. The plant provides a summerlong display of beautiful reddish pink blossoms clustered atop 15-inch spikes. It is one of the longest blooming of all perennials. One of its most unusual characteristics likens this pretty plant to a mule—of all things. Since it never sets seeds (as a mule never bears a foal), it blooms profusely. This endless attempt to reproduce itself may be confusing to the plant, but gardeners consider it a real boon. Even without its never-ending blooms, 'Luxuriant' would be worth growing for its charming filigree foliage. It also makes an enchanting, long-lasting cut flower, allowing viewers to examine its intricate blossoms at their leisure.

HOW TO GROW

Like all bleeding-hearts, 'Luxuriant' requires rich garden soil that doesn't dry out yet drains well. Increase your soil's drainage and moisture-holding capacity by digging in lots of organic matter. This plant requires little maintenance—mulch with leaf compost to retain moisture, but don't bury the crowns or they may rot.

WHERE TO GROW

'Luxuriant' is as happy in the transition zone between the sunny border and the woodland garden as it is in fairly deep shade. It doesn't like permanent shade at the north side of a building but is a great foundation plant at the northeast and northwest corners of buildings. It makes a superior ground cover, or use it in front of a border for its attractive foliage and constant color.

Top Choices

- D. 'Baccharal' has deep raspberry red flowers; it doesn't tolerate heat as well as 'Luxuriant'.

- D. 'Bountiful' also produces darker pink flowers as well as darker blue-green foliage; it holds up better under heat and sun than most varieties.

- D. 'Zestful' is similar to 'Bountiful' but with light green leaves; it has a long blooming season in milder climates.

- D. eximia 'Snowdrift' is a lovely variety with pure white flowers. Unlike its counterpart, it produces seeds and self-sows to produce a colony of offspring near the parent plant.

MAINTAINING RICH SOIL

Plants described as liking rich or fertile soil will benefit from an annual feeding (or topdressing) in addition to a year-round cover of organic mulch. Pull aside the mulch and spread an inch of aged manure or compost over plant roots; earthworms will mix this into the soil for you. If your soil tests too acidic or alkaline, this is a good time to spread a corrective dose of pH-altering amendments.

Use lime to raise pH or sulfur to lower pH. Sprinkle the amendment over the topdressing, using rates recommended on the product label. Replace mulch and rake to smooth.

OLD-FASHIONED FAVORITE

Common bleeding-heart, D. spectabilis, has been grown in gardens for centuries. Beloved by almost every gardener, it grows to 36 inches tall, with exquisite arching sprays of pink or white ('Alba') flowers. It prefers partial shade but will grow in full sun in the North, providing the soil is rich and moist. It must be kept well watered or it will turn yellow and go dormant.

FOXGLOVE
Digitalis purpurea

Zones: 4–10

Bloom Time: Late spring to early summer

Light: Part shade

Height: 4–5 ft.

Interest: Tall, elegant, pinkish purple or white flower spikes

The common foxglove is native to Europe, but it has naturalized in many parts of the Northeast and Northwest. A large grove of these stately spires in bloom in a garden or along a roadside is a truly magnificent sight. Although a short-lived perennial, foxglove seeds itself freely in favorable conditions. Once established, colonies will regenerate themselves. Foxglove is easy to grow and the sturdy flower stalks rise from low clumps of large leaves. The name *foxglove* is a corruption of *folks'-glove,* because the individual blossoms look like fingers cut from a glove. This plant, though toxic, has been used as a source of the powerful heart stimulant digitalis for over two hundred years.

HOW TO GROW

Foxglove requires rich, moist soil that doesn't dry out. The evergreen crowns resent standing water and may require winter protection (see page 17) in exposed northern areas. To increase your foxglove population, allow some spikes to produce seedpods. When stems turn brown, break open a few pods. If the seeds are brown, crush a few pods and shake the seeds onto moist, bare earth.

WHERE TO GROW

Foxglove belongs scattered in shade gardens and along shady roadsides that aren't mowed until late summer. It can also be placed in more formal borders in the shade of large shrubs or small trees. It's perfectly at home in a shaded "wild" garden. Because it is tall and the foliage at the base can look somewhat tattered toward summer's end, locate foxglove behind shorter plants.

Top Choices

- *D.* 'Excelsior Hybrids' come in mixed shades of pink, reddish purple, and white, some with heavily spotted throats. Unlike the wild plants, these produce "gloves" all around the flower stem, which can tower to 60 inches tall.

- *D.* 'Foxy' comes in mixed colors on a branching 30-inch plant and will bloom the first year from seeds sown in spring.

- *D.* 'Giant Shirley' hybrids tower to 8 or 9 feet in ideal growing conditions. They do not bloom the first year from seeds.

NATURALIZED PLANTS

Naturalized plants are those that have "escaped" from gardens to grow "naturally" in the wild without human intervention. Foxglove is a good example. Other plants that have naturalized favorably are dame's rocket, mullein, sweet William, and yellow flag iris.

Naturalization, however, sometimes turns into a severe problem, as with Scotch broom in the Northwest and purple loosestrife in northern states. Both spread rapidly by seeds and choke out native plants in natural and woodland areas.

Japanese honeysuckle and Oriental bittersweet in the mid-Atlantic states and kudzu vine in the South are vining plants that scramble over trees and buildings—and people taking long siestas—choking everything in their path. As the plants spread they crowd out many native plants that often represent the food supply for many animals. Without food these animals must also leave the area.

LEOPARD'S-BANE
Doronicum caucasicum

Zones: 4–9

Bloom Time: Spring

Light: Part shade

Height: 12–24 in.

Interest: Golden yellow daisies in early spring; heart-shaped or triangular leaves

Leopard's-bane is the perennial equivalent of the springtime favorite, forsythia. It bursts forth in all its golden glory in early spring to announce that winter is over, and is one of the first daisies to bloom. Only the true English daisy and its offspring get a head start on this decorative plant. You'll find leopard's-bane in flower when daffodils and bleeding-hearts begin to bloom. The three together are a welcome sight after the dreary grays and browns of winter—especially in cold climates. Leopard's-bane makes an excellent, long-lasting cut flower and looks terrific in a vase with the afore-mentioned spring-blooming companions. The Latin name, *Doronicum*, is derived from Arabic and perhaps the common name, which doesn't appear to relate to anything familiar to temperate-climate gardeners, comes from a similar source.

HOW TO GROW

Leopard's-bane prefers light shade, but it will grow in full sun in rich soil that holds moisture well yet never gets waterlogged. Keep the plants well watered in early summer and mulch the soil around the roots, but avoid smothering the crowns, for this may cause them to rot out. In high temperatures, the plants have a tendency to go dormant in the middle of summer, so plant annuals or dahlias in front of leopard's-bane to hide the bare earth.

WHERE TO GROW

Leopard's-bane is just as happy naturalized in a woodland with wildflowers, hostas, and ferns as it is in a mixed border. In other words, it has that ability to look informal in natural settings and formal in more cultivated surroundings. Plant lots in a cutting garden for armfuls of daisies in early spring.

Top Choices

- *D.* 'Finesse' is semidouble with larger yellowish orange flowers on sturdy 15- to 18-inch plants.

- *D.* 'Mme. Mason' blooms earlier and often blooms a second time if spent blossoms are removed. Foliage stays green longer than the species, which has a tendency to go dormant early, especially in hot, dry spells. It grows to 24 inches.

- *D.* 'Magnificum' produces larger flower heads than others and is perhaps the best selection. Plants grow to 30 inches under ideal conditions.

PLANNING AHEAD

Ephemerals are plants that disappear completely after blooming. Many spring wildflowers such as leopard's-bane and Virginia bluebells fit this description. Spring ephemerals leave a "hole" in the border when they go dormant in midsummer.

These holes are best filled with tender bulbs or annuals. However, you can't simply install these plants at the beginning of the growing season. To fill the holes, you must plan ahead, since in spring the ephemerals will occupy the space.

1 In spring, pot up impatiens, dahlias, caladiums, or similar plants in 6- to 8-inch flowerpots to give them time to get established.

2 When the spring ephemeral starts to look punky, trim yellowing foliage. (Leave the foliage in place until it has yellowed to ensure that plants will have enough energy to bloom the following spring.)

3 Hide the ephemeral with the potted filler plant placed in front.

LONGSPUR EPIMEDIUM
Epimedium grandiflorum

Zones: 5–8

Bloom Time: Spring

Light: Part shade

Height: 10–15 in.

Interest: Dainty white, yellow, and rose-violet blossoms atop pale bronze foliage

This charming perennial represents an under-used genus of rugged but delicate-looking plants with lovely flowers, very showy spring foliage, and a tough, no-nonsense ground cover habit. The spurred blossoms sit like jewels atop 10- to 15-inch foliage that is pale bronze in spring and turns greener in summer. Cut a few for a vase in the kitchen windowsill, where you can enjoy their delightful form up close for days.

HOW TO GROW
The key to success with longspur epimedium is soil preparation (as it is with almost every plant). It must have rich, organic soil that remains moist, but never stays wet. Once the plant is well established, it can tolerate some drought but will need watering during long dry spells. It requires only an annual trimming to

ground level in early spring before new foliage starts to grow; reapply mulch at the same time.

WHERE TO GROW

Epimedium is an extremely versatile plant in most shady situations. It is suitable for individual plantings in a rock garden or by a path at the foot of a tree. It's also perfect for use in large sweeps as a ground cover under trees or large shrubs, or as a foundation plant. Once plants fill in (which can take a while), they'll keep out most weeds. Epemedium is an unusual container plant for shady decks or patios, especially good for providing spring interest in combination with bulbs.

Top Choices

- *E.* 'Lilac Fairy', 'White Queen' ('Snow Queen'), and 'Rose Queen' ('Lilafee') have flowers of white-tipped violet, white, and rose, respectively. All grow 10 to 15 inches tall.

- *E.* x *perralchicum* 'Frohnleiten' has yellow blossoms on 8- to 12-inch plants and tolerates dryness better than other epimediums.

- *E.* x *rubrum*, red epimedium, has bright red flowers; its large leaves are brushed with red in spring. Zones 4 to 8.

- *E.* x *versicolor* 'Sulphureum' has pale yellow flowers and is especially cold hardy. Zones 4 to 8.

GARDENING IN DRY SHADE

It isn't surprising to find pockets of dry shade under densely canopied trees, in shaded areas above thirsty shrub or tree roots, under wide eaves or patio overhangs, and in shaded, fast-draining soil. You can take three approaches to gardening in these difficult sites:

- First, amend the soil with a moisture-retentive material. Use well-aged manure or compost, shredded peat moss, leaf mold, or a locally available organic product such as apple pomace, mushroom compost, or buckwheat or rice hulls. (If the materials are not completely composted, you need to fortify your soil with a slow-release nitrogen fertilizer.)

- Second, select plants such as epimedium that thrive in dry, shaded sites. Bleeding-heart, lilyturf, spotted dead nettle, and periwinkle are a few other shade lovers that survive with limited water.

- And finally, place a layer of mulch over the soil surface after planting to hold in the moisture and cut down on evaporation.

SWEET WOODRUFF
Galium odoratum

Zones: 4–9

Bloom Time: Spring and early summer

Light: Part to full shade

Height: 4–9 in.

Interest: A useful ground cover with spring green leaves and twinkling white flowers

Sweet woodruff is a delightful little plant with soft green leaves the color of spring. The narrow leaves grow in a whorl (like the spokes of an umbrella) around square stems, creating a more delicate texture than most ground covers. The tiny white starlike blossoms sparkle above the foliage in spring and early summer and have a delicate fragrance. When crushed, this sweet-smelling plant has the scent of new-mown hay. (The aroma comes from coumarin, a chemical used by the perfume industry to help fix fragrances.) Added to wine, this herb creates that unique and delicious libation—*Maibowle*, or spring wine. Sweet woodruff is a bewitching plant that makes a useful ground cover in shady locations, where it spreads freely and only rarely becomes a pest.

HOW TO GROW

Plant in well-drained, woodsy soil that retains moisture. Mulch thinly in early spring to maintain the organic content of the soil and hold in moisture. Provide water during long dry spells to keep the foliage from browning. Sweet woodruff requires no other care, not even cutting back. You can divide clumps to increase your supply at any time during the growing season. To keep it from spreading beyond a certain point, drive a sharp spade into the ground at the desired edge of the clump and pull up any runners beyond the cut boundary.

WHERE TO GROW

A shade garden without sweet woodruff is hardly worth contemplating. It will fit anywhere and everywhere, with wildflowers, with cultivated woodland treasures, or as a ground cover under shrubs and trees. As a ground cover, it mixes well with spring- or summer-flowering bulbs and lilies. Cut a few sprigs to accompany lily-of-the-valley in a dainty late-spring bouquet.

Top Choice

- *G. verum,* lady's bedstraw, tolerates drier soils, grows to 3 feet tall, and produces sweet-smelling yellow flowers. Historically, it was used as a fragrant stuffing for mattresses—hence its common name.

PRESSING PERENNIALS

Pressing flowers between the pages of a book is a quick and simple way to preserve blooms from the garden. But to prepare longer-lasting remembrances for mounting or framing, you'll want to take a few special steps:

1 Choose a blossom with a single row of petals and a small center. (You may need to flatten a rounded center with your thumb and forefinger while it's still moist.) Collect a bud along with the flower as well as a stem with a leaf or two attached for a complete picture of the plant.

2 Place all the pieces in a single layer between two pieces of blotting paper, smooth paper towels, or newspaper. You can lay the flower directly inside an old telephone book if you don't mind that bleeding colors may damage the print.

3 Place the papers between flat, heavy surfaces, such as large books, that you can easily move to check the drying process. As moisture is absorbed from the flower and leaves, you'll need to replace the original sheets of paper with dry ones. If the paper is especially thin or the plants are large and fleshy, use several sheets. It usually takes four to six weeks before your perennial is truly everlasting.

BLOODY CRANESBILL
Geranium sanguineum

Zones: 4–7

Bloom Time: Summer

Light: Part shade

Height: 10–15 in.

Interest: Intense reddish purple flowers; delicate mounds of dark green, lacy foliage

The bloody cranesbill is a true perennial geranium (unlike the commonly grown red geranium more properly called *Pelargonium*). This geranium has an intense color that dominates its neighbors when in flower. Its color isn't to everyone's taste, but it makes a strong statement for gardeners who like bright colors. The leaves are small and lacy, produced in such numbers that the low-growing plants appear dense. The plant spreads to three to four times its height, making it an excellent choice for a ground cover. It also boasts a longer bloom time than most perennials.

HOW TO GROW
Bloody cranesbill prefers average garden soil. It is more tolerant of drought than other cranesbills and many other shade plants. It will also grow in moist soil, but

not in areas where water stands. It requires little or no maintenance. To increase your supply, look for small seedlings near the parent plant in spring or dig up and divide clumps in early spring. Bloody cransesbill can tolerate western heat but not the heat and humidity of the Deep South.

WHERE TO GROW

Use this versatile geranium in almost any garden wherever a low-growing, colorful plant or delicate leaf texture is needed. Position it at the front of a border or at the edge of a woodland path. Due to its strong color, it is best planted beside foliage plants such as ferns, hostas, and Jack-in-the-pulpits, or alongside plants with white blossoms such as sweet woodruff, dwarf goatsbeard, and foamflower. It blends well with the pale pink blossoms of its refined relative *G. sanguineum* var. *striatum*.

Top Choices

- G. 'Alpenglow' is similar to the species but has a profusion of larger flowers.

- G. *macrorrhizum*, bigroot geranium, is noted for its pungently fragrant foliage on 15- to 18-inch stems. 'Ingwersen's Variety' is a choice pale pink selection. Zones 4 to 9.

- G. *sanguineum* var. *striatum* is slightly lower growing. It is an exquisite pale shade of pink with delicate, deep rose veins. The flowers blend well with almost every color. It is sometimes sold as 'Lancastriense'.

CREATING COLOR-CLASH GROUPINGS

In recent years, a few gardens have featured extraordinary color-clash borders, where plants are put together in combinations that are jarring to traditional eyes. When seen as a whole, plantings like these have a pop-art appearance—and are striking to say the least.

To try a similar effect in your garden, start with bloody cranesbill—it's easy to find plants with which it will clash. Then underplant it with late-flowering orange and baby pink tulips—you're sure to need sunglasses to view this bold combination of colors.

For added drama, and to extend the color contrast through the season, include some plants with purple or chartreuse foliage. Consider the new coralbell cultivars such as 'Montrose Ruby' that offer purple foliage with attractive patterning that remains good looking all season. For chartreuse foliage, try hostas such as 'Sum and Substance' or 'August Moon', or golden hakone grass (*Hakonechloa macro* 'Aureola').

LENTEN ROSE
Helleborus orientalis

Zones: 4–10

Bloom Time: Early spring

Light: Part to full shade

Height: 18–24 in.

Interest: Pink, rosy purple, dark maroon, green, or white flowers; attractive evergreen foliage

Lenten rose is a wonderful ornamental plant that deserves a place in every shade garden the year round. The 2- to 4-inch-wide, nodding blossoms come in a pleasing array of colors; some have spots inside the blooms. Because the showy parts of the flowers are the sepals, instead of the petals, they remain attractive for weeks. The dark evergreen foliage is ornamental all year, especially in mild climates and when sheltered from icy winds in northern climates. Lenten rose is a tough plant that usually self-sows. When planted with different shades, it produces pleasing color variations. Many new extraordinary shades are available due to the recent intensive breeding, especially in Britain. Since lenten rose is notoriously slow to reproduce vegetatively, mixed seedlings from this rich new gene pool are all that are readily available.

HOW TO GROW

Lenten rose is the easiest of the hellebore clan to grow. It thrives in less-than-ideal conditions, but flourishes best in soil rich in organic matter so that it holds moisture but never stays waterlogged. The plants will tolerate part and full shade, which makes them even more useful. They seed themselves freely unless you remove the spent blooms before the seedpods turn brown and burst open. In the North, the foliage remains attractive in winter only if sheltered from cold winds by hedges, solid fences, or woody evergreens (such as hemlock or mountain laurel).

WHERE TO GROW

Lenten rose loves shade—in woodland gardens, along garden pathways, and at building foundations. Use it by the house in place of overused traditional ground covers for long-lasting, glossy greenery. It also makes an excellent cut flower. Scatter seeds or transplant seedlings in the "back forty" to have extra plants for cutting.

Top Choices

- *H. foetidus*, bear's foot, is a very attractive plant with unusual green flowers on 18- to 24-inch stalks. Zones 3 to 10.

- *H. niger*, Christmas rose, is one of the earliest plants to flower—even at Christmastime in mild climates. Its pure white blossoms fade to pink as they age. Plants grow 8 to 12 inches tall with attractive green foliage but are somewhat temperamental. Zones 3 to 8.

PETAL, SEPAL, OR TEPAL?

In some plants the showy parts of the flower are called petals. They are sepals in others. So what's the difference?

To most gardeners there is no practical difference between a petal and a sepal, and if it looks like a flower then the pretty parts are called petals, period. To botanists, however, flowers are not quite that simple. It turns out that the difference between petals and sepals is all in location.

Flowers are composed of a series of parts arranged one atop the other. On some plants, the sepals are small and green and look like little leaves. On others, they are large and nicely colored and look more like flower petals. Collectively the sepals are called the calyx. Just above the sepals are the petals.

On some plants, such as the hellebores, there are no flower petals at all and the sepals provide the color and interest.

On other plants, such as tulips, alliums, and many lilies, the petals and sepals are nearly indistinguishable—they are the same size, shape, and color. Together they are called tepals.

CORALBELLS
Heuchera sanguinea

Zones: 3–10

Bloom Time: Late spring and all summer

Light: Part shade

Height: 12–18 in.

Interest: Coral-red flowers on thin, delicate-looking stems; attractive foliage

Coralbells is an easy-to-grow, rosy-flowered species. A cottage-garden favorite, it is also the proud parent of many exciting new varieties hybridized in recent years. Its tiny coral-red blossoms wave on thin stems above lobed, kidney-shaped leaves. The foliage provides a pleasant background for the showy flower spikes and remains attractive all season. Much of the recent breeding work with this species has focused either on developing plants with showier flowers or plants with ornamental evergreen foliage. Next will come plants with both brilliantly colored flowers and striking foliage.

HOW TO GROW

All coralbells require moist but well-drained, rich, organic soil, close to neutral pH. Before planting, dig in lots of leaf compost. Where soils are naturally acidic, also dig in some dolomitic limestone to make them sweet. Mulch with leaf compost, keeping it away from the crowns to avoid encouraging rot. Water well during dry spells. The flowers of most of the varieties grown for foliage are not especially attractive and may be removed as soon as they appear. Divide in early spring to maintain vigor.

WHERE TO GROW

Coralbells belong in both perennial borders and woodland gardens, in formal situations and informal plantings. To appreciate their wandlike blossoms, position them near the edge of the border or along a path or shady walkway. Although the blooms are held high, the thin stems are almost transparent, so they will not block the view of plants behind them. After bloom, the tidy clumps of foliage stay quite low to the ground

Top Choices

The following are hybrid varieties (*H.* x *brizoides,* also listed as *H. sanguinea*) known for their flowers. They grow 18 to 24 inches tall. Zones 4 to 10.

- *H.* 'Bressingham' hybrids are variable, seed-grown strains of *H.* x *brizoides* in mixed shades of red and pink.

- *H.* 'Coral Cloud' is a lovely coral-pink.

- *H.* 'June Bride' is a vigorous grower with large, pure white flowers.

- *H.* 'Mt. St. Helens' has long-lasting, cherry red flowers.

CORALBELLS AS FOLIAGE PLANTS

Recently, much effort has been devoted to breeding coralbell cultivars that offer particularly attractive foliage. 'Palace Purple', a purple-leafed plant that originated at Kew Gardens, was largely responsible for this trend. There are so many from which to choose, but consider the ones in the following list for starters. While these cultivars produce blooms, they tend to be small and white to cream colored, not nearly as showy as those developed for their flowers. But the dramatic foliage provides color in the garden for the whole growing season, much longer than flowers could.

- H. 'Chocolate Ruffles' has chocolate-bronze, 9-inch leaves that are highly ruffled.

- H. 'Molly Bush', a superb selection with deep purple leaves, was developed from 'Palace Purple'.

- H. 'Montrose Ruby' offers deep red leaves with silver variegation; it tolerates more sun and drought than others.

- H. 'Pewter Veil' has pink and bronze accents on its pewter gray foliage, which shows up well in dark corners.

- H. 'Sterling Silver' is marked with blue and purple veining.

PLANTAIN LILY

Hosta

Zones: 3–9

Bloom Time: Early summer

Light: Part shade

Height: 6–36 in.

Interest: Beautiful variegated leaves; white or pale lavender blossoms

Hostas have become the perennial of choice for the shade garden, prized for their beautiful and richly textured foliage. No other plant is as attractive or as versatile in combination with other plants. Hostas are hands-down winners for their low maintenance and for their ability to outcompete weeds, not to mention for introducing more shades of blue and green foliage into the garden than any other plant! Colors range from forest green, chartreuse, and yellow to bluish green and grayish blue. Some cultivars are variegated at the leaf margins or with a central flame pattern in white, cream, or yellow. In the past two or three decades, hostas have been hybridized and selected to produce thousands of named varieties. Though sometimes overlooked, hosta blossoms make excellent cut flowers. Some varieties are exquisitely fragrant.

How to Grow

'Frances Williams' prefers light morning sun and afternoon shade, but will grow in almost full sun (except in the South) if given rich soil and constant moisture. Leaves will burn if given too much sun, but some bright, indirect light intensifies the variegation of the foliage and increases flowering. If you prefer foliage only, simply remove the flower stalks. Divide clumps only when they become overcrowded. (See "Where to Grow" on page 62.)

Top Choices

- *H.* 'Aurora Borealis' is nearly identical to 'Frances Williams' but with brighter and more puckered leaves; its flowers are white.

- *H.* 'Frances Williams' has been considered one of the finest varieties for over sixty years and is still the standard by which many new selections are measured. It has large, nearly round, blue-green leaves that are puckered and slightly cupped with leaf edges rimmed in greenish gold. Plants spread to an amazing 4 feet across, reach 3 feet in height, and are topped by pale lavender blossoms inlate summer.

- *H. sieboldiana* 'Elegans' has large, grayish blue leaves and nearly white flowers. It is more robust than 'Frances Williams'.

- *H.* 'Sum and Substance' has huge chartreuse leaves and lavender flowers; it needs some light to bring out the beauty of its foliage and will tolerate up to a half day of sun.

Maintaining HOSTA FOLIAGE

Hosta foliage is remarkably handsome and nearly maintenance-free. It looks best when you protect it against pests and provide a balance of sun and shade.

Slugs and snails are especially fond of hosta leaves. They leave behind long, ragged holes and silvery gray trails. You can keep their damage to a minimum or prevent it altogether by setting out bait or handpicking. (See page 35 for other methods of control.)

Sunscald causes unsightly gray to tan blisters or bleached areas on the upper leaf surfaces. These spots often enlarge, creating large lesions or papery-thin, dried tissue. Variegated varieties in full sun are the most susceptible. Blue-leafed hostas fade to green if they don't get enough shade.

Keep hostas looking lush by cutting off severely damaged foliage at ground level. New leaves will soon regenerate if plants are well watered. For best appearance, topdress with compost or douse the soil with diluted fish emulsion.

FRAGRANT HOSTA
Hosta plantaginea

Zones: 3–9

Bloom Time: Late summer

Light: Part shade

Height: 18 in.

Interest: Beautiful light green leaves; fragrant white blossoms

Called fragrant hosta for its scented white blossoms, this late-summer bloomer is one of the oldest and most popular of the cultivated hostas. (It was previously known as August lily.) Prized for their ornamental value in the garden, the blossoms also make excellent cut flowers. Fragrant hosta is most popular for its large, upright, trumpet-shaped blossoms, but it is always welcome in the garden for its bright green foliage. The glossy leaves are 8 to 10 inches long and 6 to 8 inches wide on plants that grow 18 inches tall by 2 feet wide.

WHERE TO GROW
Where rainfall is plentiful in summer, most landscapes in temperate climates have a site for this and other hostas. The lush foliage fits easily into shrub and perennial borders and is widely used as an accent among foundation

plants, around the base of a tree, or scattered throughout low ground covers on banks or near lawns. In humid northern climates, you can grow fragrant hosta in full sun as long as the soil stays adequately moist. Where heavy soil is soggy from winter rains, plant on raised mounds for better drainage; the dormant crowns suffer from wet conditions.

Fragrant hosta foliage combines well with other shade-loving plants, especially smooth-leafed lilies and grasses and anything with variegated leaves. Partner pale, glossy-leafed hostas with highly textured astilbes and ferns; variegated types look best planted with other solid green foliage. (See "How to Grow" on page 61.)

Top Choices

- *H.* 'Fragrant Blue' forms tight mounds of heart-shaped, powder blue leaves topped by lightly scented, pale lilac blooms.

- *H.* 'Honeybells' is closely related to the fragrant lily. It has yellowish green leaves and fragrant, pale violet flowers.

- *H.* 'Royal Standard' is a vigorous hybrid with deeply veined, pale green leaves and abundant, scented, large white flowers.

- *H.* 'So Sweet' forms upright clumps of green leaves trimmed with wide margins of cream. Abundant, very fragrant flowers are nearly white.

TIPS FOR HOSTA CULTURE

As shade lovers, more hostas are planted under trees than in any other location. When you select a hosta variety, keep in mind its planting location and the habits of the trees above.

- Some trees are messy and tend to drop litter such as blossom petals after their late-spring or summer bloom. Deeply veined and highly puckered hosta foliage often seems to hold these droppings more readily than smoother-leafed types.

- Position hostas in rings around trees so that moisture doesn't accumulate at the base of the tree, causing a fungus problem. Allow at least 1 foot between the edges of the mature, arching foliage and the tree trunk.

- Look for dense growth when you buy new hostas so you'll end up with enough for a mass planting at a very low cost.

- Separate the young shoots of a densely filled nursery container, pot them separately, and let them grow for a year before setting them into the garden.

- Divide hostas only when they're overcrowded—about once every five years—in early spring. With a sharp spade, dig through the crown and root mass, lift out a section, and replant.

CRESTED IRIS
Iris cristata

Zones: 3–9

Bloom Time: Spring

Light: Part shade

Height: 4–8 in.

Interest: Delightful blue flowers on short plants; arching, soft, green leaves like large blades of grass

The crested iris is a choice dwarf that adapts well to cultivation. It has sparkling, sweetly scented 2-inch blossoms that vary from pale to deep lilac blue, with darker blue and white markings and a yellow crest. Though short, the exquisite flowers show up remarkably well among the dwarf iris leaves. There are selections with dark blue or white flowers also with a yellow crest. This perennial makes a fine little ground cover—it spreads slowly but steadily, running along the ground with small creeping rhizomes. After it finishes blooming, it remains a tidy but dense forest of miniature iris leaves.

HOW TO GROW
This tough little plant grows well in shade or full sun, if planted in rich, well-drained, organic soil that doesn't stay too wet or too dry. When planting, don't cover the

tops of the small rhizomes with soil or they will rot. Water well during dry spells. In a border, crested iris will soon outgrow its position, so divide it after a few years and place the surplus plants in the woods where they can wander at will. It is prey to slugs, which devour the delicate blooms like candy. (See page 35 for how to get rid of this pest.)

WHERE TO GROW

This dainty-looking yet rugged plant is equally happy in part to light shade; the more sun it gets, the more soil moisture it needs. Crested iris is a charming plant to place amid other wildflowers or beneath shrubs in a more formal mixed border. Try it too at the edge of a perennial border for late-spring color. It also deserves a spot in shady rock gardens.

Top Choices

- *I.* 'Alba' is a dazzling pure white form.

- *I.* 'Summer Storm' has darker flowers than the species, a rich, deep blue-violet.

- *I. tectorum,* Japanese roof iris, is very similar to the crested iris, but about two to three times its size. Zones 5 to 9.

AVOIDING THE IRIS BORER

Iris borers are night-flying moths that emerge in late summer and land on iris leaves to lay their eggs. The eggs overwinter and hatch in early spring. The green caterpillars tunnel into the iris leaves just above the crown of the plant. As they eat their way to and then devour the inside of the rhizome, the caterpillars become fat, pink worms.

Iris borers are perfectly capable of destroying irises all on their own, but in some instances they do more damage by spreading disease. Bacterial soft rot—which is spread by iris borers—destroys the rhizome, turning it into a smelly mess.

To avoid iris borers and bacterial soft rot, follow these guidelines:

❶ Cut back iris leaves and flower stalks to the ground in fall. This will destroy the eggs laid by the moths in late summer.

❷ If borers are seen in spring, dig up the affected plants and cut out the infested portions using a sharp knife. (Sharp cuts are less apt to invite disease.) Dip the remaining rhizome in a solution of 1 part bleach and 3 parts water, and replant.

❸ Avoid planting iris in the area that was infested for at least five to six years.

SPOTTED DEAD NETTLE
Lamium maculatum

Zones: 4–10

Bloom Time: Late spring to summer

Light: Part to full shade

Height: 12–15 in.

Interest: Colorful, very easy-to-grow ground cover

Despite its rather unappealing colloquial name (it lacks the rash-producing hairs of the rather nasty stinging nettle), spotted dead nettle is a superior ground cover. It is dead-easy to grow, it spreads without being invasive, and its purplish red flowers provide color all season long. Its small attractive green leaves are marked with a central band of silver-gray. There are also selections with silver-gray foliage edged in gray-green and others with showy pink, violet, or white flowers. In northern gardens, spotted dead nettle is one of the few plants that will tolerate dry shade.

HOW TO GROW
Spotted dead nettle will grow in almost any soil type (but not wet) and any amount of shade. It does best in rich, well-mulched garden soil (keep the mulch away from the

crown to avoid diseases). After flowering, shear the plants to produce a new flush of vigorous growth. In the South plants must be well watered and sheared occasionally to keep them looking tidy. Spotted dead nettle is easy to propagate; anytime you want to increase your supply, simply root stem cuttings or dig up rooted runners and replant.

WHERE TO GROW

Grow spotted dead nettle wherever you need a ground cover—under trees or shrubs, along the edge of a shady driveway, with evergreen foundation plants, or to add color in shady areas. Plant it as a delicate textural contrast under large hostas, too. Since it tolerates dry shade better than most ground covers, spotted dead nettle can be used to replace sparse lawn under trees (and reduce your mowing chores).

Top Choices

- *L.* 'Beacon Silver' has pinkish purple flowers that sit above silver-white foliage edged in grayish green.

- *L.* 'Chequers' is characterized by rich violet-pink flowers and green leaves with a slender silver stripe.

- *L.* 'Pink Pewter' is another lovely selection with large pink flowers and silver-gray leaves, edged in grayish green.

- *L.* 'White Nancy' is similar to 'Pink Pewter' but has pure white flowers and is one of the most attractive and vigorous selections.

PROPAGATION FROM STEM CUTTINGS

Rooting stem cuttings is an easy form of vegetative propagation when plants grow roots easily. It's often easier to get more clumps using this method than by dividing existing clumps. Try it with spotted dead nettle, periwinkle, and upright bugle, to name a few.

1 Remove the lower pair of leaves from 4- to 6-inch nonflowering shoots. Stick the cut ends of the shoots in a glass of water on a sunless windowsill. Allow the shoots to develop roots for four to six weeks.

2 Transplant the shoots to the desired outdoor location and water thoroughly. Cover with weighted-down newspaper for a few days to shade them.

3 Remove the newspaper for a short time in the morning or late afternoon; increase the time by a little each day, until the new plants are perky enough to stand on their own.

BIGLEAF GOLDENRAY

Ligularia dentata

Zones: 4–8

Bloom Time: Summer

Light: Part shade

Height: 36–48 in.

Interest: Showy orange-yellow flowers; bold ornamental foliage

Bigleaf goldenray is a large, imposing plant with yellow to orange blossoms in flat-topped, well-branched clusters. It is grown partly for its huge, kidney-shaped leaves up to 20 inches wide; in some cultivars, the foliage is strikingly dark. The bright orange-yellow flower heads measure 2 to 5 inches across. It demands deep, moist soil that never dries out—conditions that can be difficult to find in parts of the Southeast and Southwest.

HOW TO GROW

Bigleaf goldenray must have moist soil; otherwise it wilts dramatically and looks decidedly unhappy. If the location you have in mind is not naturally moist, add lots of organic matter such as leaf compost or peat moss to the soil before planting. Mulch with a thick layer of leaf compost, pine needles, or shredded pine bark, and water heavily during dry spells. Unfortunately, this plant loves the same moist, humus-rich conditions as slugs and snails, and these slimy pests can make inroads in the leaves. (To control slugs, see page 35.)

WHERE TO GROW

Place bigleaf goldenray to make a bold statement by a pond, alongside a stream, or at the edge of a swampy area. In constantly wet soil, this plant will grow in full sun; otherwise it must have part shade. Plant in combination with other vigorous foliage plants such as large-leafed hosta, umbrella plant, or giant butterbur. It is one of the few shade plants that offer yellow to orange flowers, so use it when you want to add this color to a planting scheme or to brighten an otherwise dark spot. Bigleaf goldenray is a bold plant in color and stature; it needs companion plants of similar size that are also vigorous growers so they won't be overwhelmed and overrun.

Top Choices

- *L.* 'Desdemona' and 'Othello' have stunning, dark purple-maroon foliage and are more handsome than the species. 'Othello' is more compact.

- *L. stenocephala* 'The Rocket' is grown primarily for its very showy, 48- to 60-inch-tall, narrow spikes of golden yellow flowers on dark stems; its toothed leaves are a basic green.

SPACING LARGE PLANTS

When planting large plants such as bigleaf goldenray, it's sometimes difficult to remember that the small specimen in the nursery pot will mature into a much bigger plant. For best long-term results, space large plants with the following planting tips in mind:

- Be sure to follow the spacing recommendations on the nursery tag so your plant has room to expand to its full potential.

- If there's no tag, here's a good rule of thumb. Find out (from this book, nursery staff, or the mail-order catalog from which you ordered) the expected mature height of the plant. Divide this height in half, and space plants at least this distance apart.

- Be patient. It may take plants two or more years to fill out into their full size. If you want to fill the space between young plants for the first year or two, use annuals such as impatiens or coleus.

LILYTURF
Liriope muscari

Zones: 6–10

Bloom Time: Late summer

Light: Part shade

Height: 12–18 in.

Interest: Handsome evergreen ground cover with broad-leafed, grasslike foliage; lilac-blue or white blossoms

Lilyturf's tolerance for varying light conditions and its drought resistance makes it indispensable in the home landscape and for commercial plantings. It is a tough, problem-free, evergreen ground cover that remains attractive year-round. Variegated selections provide even more ornamental value. The flowers look like grape hyacinths and bloom pure white or in pale or deep shades of lilac-blue.

HOW TO GROW

Lilyturf isn't too fussy about light conditions but it definitely resents standing in water. Like spotted dead nettle (see page 66), it is one of the few plants that thrive in dry shade. Mow down the foliage in late winter or early spring just before the new leaves emerge to keep the plants looking fresh each spring. Where winters are mild, spring renewal may not be necessary if plants don't look tired or tattered. For more plants, divide established clumps in spring. Lilyturf is rarely troubled by diseases or pests—other than slugs and snails.

WHERE TO GROW

Plant lilyturf in shade or sun, wherever a tidy ground cover is desired. It looks its best when planted in large sweeps with different varieties swirled together. Its grasslike form looks equally good in urban courtyards, edging suburban entrys, or in rural gardens. Variegated forms add significant garden interest, even when not in bloom.

Top Choices

- *L.* 'Gold Banded' has deep green leaves with a narrow gold band down each side. Plants grow to 18 inches tall.

- *L.* 'Monroe White' has dense, pure white flower spikes and deep green leaves.

- *L.* 'Silvery Sunproof' is a striking selection with abundant lilac flowers and almost white leaves on 15-inch plants. The stripes are more yellow in shade.

- *L.* 'Variegata' is the most popular variety and has deep lilac flowers on 20-inch plants with cream-edged leaves that are more yellow when they first appear.

UNDERPLANTING GROUND COVERS

To prevent ground covers planted in large groups from looking boring, try these ideas:

- Underplant with spring- and summer-flowering bulbs. Daffodil mixtures (*Narcissus* varieties) are ideal for this purpose, because as they provide extended spring color and grow happily in a variety of conditions. Daffodils grow especially well beneath deciduous trees, where they receive plentiful spring sun and summer shade.

- For summer color, underplant with true lilies (*Lilium* varieties). Asiatic lilies add a burst of midsummer color and Oriental lilies are late-summer bloomers; use both for a long season of color. Lilies require some sun to bloom, so choose a spot with light dappled shade (the sunniest spot in your ground cover planting).

- Perhaps the easiest plants to mingle with ground covers are hybrid daylilies (*Hemerocallis* varieties). While not true lilies (or bulbs), daylilies also blend well with all sorts of ground covers, provide summer flowers, and bloom well in light shade.

VIRGINIA BLUEBELLS
Mertensia virginica

Zones: 3–9

Bloom Time: Spring

Light: Part to full shade

Height: 15–24 in.

Interest: Delightful blue flowers in spring; apple green foliage

Virginia bluebells is a much-loved eastern native that produces clusters of nodding fragrant blossoms. Soft blue flowers begin as pink buds and often retain a faint blush of the bud color. The leaves emerge a distinctive bluish green shade before maturing into bright apple green. Virginia bluebells is a spring ephemeral—it blossoms in spring and goes dormant in the heat of summer. That means you need to plan for the hole it will leave behind. It is best combined with later-developing plants such as hostas, ferns, or shade-loving annuals; these will expand enough by midsummer to fill in the spaces left by this charming plant. (Also see "Planning Ahead," page 49.) Virginia bluebells is very easy to grow and requires little or no maintenance. Keep it happy and it will self-sow freely, but never invasively.

HOW TO GROW

Virginia bluebells prefers humus-rich soil that retains moisture but is well drained. To help the soil hold moisture and provide a prime site for self-sown seeds to germinate, mulch well with leaf compost in late winter, before the new growth emerges. Since the leaves yellow as they go dormant, you may want to plant bluebells with larger, later-developing plants to camouflage the less-than-lovely discoloring foliage. Otherwise, you may wish to cut the plants down at bloom's end.

To increase your planting, wait until the foliage has turned yellow, cut off the stems, and shake the plants over bare, humus-rich earth to scatter the seeds. The fleshy roots are brittle and are easily broken, so seeds are generally more successful than dividing to increase your stock. If relocation is necessary, the best time to do it is as the foliage goes dormant in late spring to early summer. Buy container-grown plants rather than collecting from the wild. They'll have a much better chance of survival and you won't disturb the natural plant community.

WHERE TO GROW

To see Virginia bluebells dangling alongside a woodland path is one of the great joys of spring. Plant it also under trees or large shrubs. It looks at home combined with other native spring ephemerals such as violet, spring beauty, mayapple, Eastern trout lily, and merrybells, as well as with "exotics" such as daffodil, bleeding-heart, and leopard's-bane.

MULCHING

Mulch holds in moisture, adds organic matter to the soil, and keeps weeds in check. Mulching for winter protection requires a different strategy (page 17).

- Use coarse mulch to keep weeds from self-sowing. However, it will also reduce the number of seedlings of desirable self-sown plants.

- Mulch in fall after cutting back the stems or in early spring as plants emerge so you can determine where the crowns are and avoid mulching them.

- To smother weeds between desirable plants, cut weeds short and lay ten to twelve newspaper pages between plants. Disguise with 3 to 4 inches of mulch.

- Avoid lightweight mulch that can blow away in the wind—it is almost impossible to rake leaves off in fall and leaf-blowers play havoc with it.

- Do not use peat moss as a mulch; it dries to form a crusty surface that repels water.

BLUE-EYED MARY
Omphalodes verna

Zones: 5–9

Bloom Time: Spring

Light: Part shade

Height: 6–8 in.

Interest: Starry blue, forget-me-not-like flowers; tidy, dark green foliage on a compact ground cover

Although blue-eyed Mary is a native of southern Europe, it is perfectly hardy in much of the United States. It is a pretty little plant with startlingly blue flowers that look like forget-me-nots and clean, dark green foliage that is evergreen in mild areas. It is tolerant of poor soils and somewhat dry conditions and spreads by underground shoots, making it a very useful, low-maintenance ground cover. It is said to have been a favorite flower of Marie Antoinette—hence its common name. Another common name, creeping forget-me-not, comes from its resemblance to the true forget-me-not, a cousin.

HOW TO GROW
Blue-eyed Mary must be grown in part shade. It will tolerate a wide variety of soil conditions though it prefers moist, humus-rich soil like most shade lovers.

Before planting, add lots of organic matter—leaf compost or peat moss—and mulch with leaf compost, pine needles, or shredded pine bark. In dry shade blue-eyed Mary requires frequent watering. Slugs and snails can be a problem in damp locations (see page 35). You can grow this plant from seeds or propagate by dividing existing clumps in either spring or fall.

WHERE TO GROW

To appreciate the delicate beauty of blue-eyed Mary's flowers, you must see them up close. Plant this low-growing plant in patches at the edge of a path through woodland areas or along the main entryway for early color. More colorful than many ground covers, it can still be used the same way as a pleasing partner to spring-blooming bulbs such as pink-cupped or pale yellow varieties of daffodils. Place it in a large container with a few daffodil bulbs in fall and put them close to a kitchen door; give them both a new home in the woods after they both bloom.

Top Choices

- O. *cappadocica* is similar to blue-eyed Mary, but more compact. It tolerates drier soil.

- O. 'Starry Eyes' is a showier, sparkling selection with a white halo around the outer edges of the bright blue petals.

Garden Companions

Pair the cheerful sprays of blue-eyed Mary with other blue-flowering species or mix them in with plants with pastel blooms of pink, white, or yellow:

- CELANDINE POPPY
- CHRISTMAS ROSE
- CRESTED IRIS
- DWARF GOATSBEARD
- EPIMEDIUM
- EUROPEAN GINGER
- LILY-OF-THE-VALLEY
- WILD BLUE PHLOX
- YELLOW CORYDALIS

OVERPLANTINGS FOR BULBS

Spring-blooming bulbs dazzle with their perky blossoms until the foliage fades, leaving empty spaces in beds and borders. You can avoid unsightly gaps in your garden by overplanting bulbs with spreading, leafy covers that also bloom, such as blue-eyed Mary, forget-me-not, viola, or pansy. More aggressive covers (myrtle, pachysandra, ajuga, and bishop's weed) can outcompete your bulbs and cause them to stop flowering after a few years or to die out completely.

PACHYSANDRA
Pachysandra terminalis

Zones: 5–9

Bloom Time: Spring

Light: Part to full shade

Height: 8–12 in.

Interest: Evergreen ground cover

Common pachysandra probably needs no introduction. This Japanese plant is the most widely planted ground cover in the United States because it is durable, fast growing, attractive, and evergreen. Pachysandra has rich emerald green foliage year-round; its unspectacular white flowers appear in late spring. It spreads by underground shoots and, once established, runs sideways with great abandon, choking out all but the strongest of companions. When grown in deep shade, it is unsurpassed for carpeting the ground with foliage.

HOW TO GROW
Pachysandra will tolerate a wide variety of soil conditions, but it grows best and most vigorously if planted in soil rich in organic matter that will retain moisture. If planted in poorer soil, it will take longer to fill in. Once

established it requires no maintenance. To start new plantings, just dig up clumps of plants from a large patch, making certain to get the underground shoots. Plant in good rich soil, then mulch and water well until the new transplants are established.

WHERE TO GROW

Use pachysandra wherever a tough plant is needed in shady locations to cover the earth with green foliage. A wide expanse of it looks much more attractive than the sparse lawn that often struggles under trees. Use to visually tie together trees in a lawn and to eliminate the need to trim grass around the tree trunks.

Top Choices

- *P.* 'Green Carpet' is a more compact selection with darker-colored leaves and better cold hardiness. Zones 4 to 9.

- *P.* 'Silveredge' has green leaves edged with silvery white. It is an interesting variation on the all-green theme. Less vigorous, it must be kept away from plantings of the species, which will choke it out.

- *P. procumbens,* Allegheny spurge, is the native American pachysandra, a much-underused plant. It has large, marbled leaves and showy white spring flowers, tinged with pink. A more refined plant than its Japanese relative, it spreads much more slowly and looks best when planted with other spring-flowering wildflowers.

PLANTING GROUND COVERS

Prepare the soil for ground covers just as you would if you were planting a lawn. Remove both the roots and aboveground parts of any grass or weeds, loosen the soil, add amendments if you need them, and rake the surface smooth.

Set plants in holes so they're at the same depth as they were in the nursery containers. Plants like pachysandra grow fast and can be spaced about 12 inches apart. When you space them evenly in a triangular arrangement, individual plants will be offset in parallel rows and will have a neat look as they fill in.

Ground covers over large areas look best if interplanted with occasional clumps of other equally vigorous plants to break up the monotony. You can use large hostas, tall ferns, shrubs, or small trees.

UMBRELLA PLANT
Peltiphyllum peltatum

Zones: 5–9

Bloom Time: Early spring

Light: Part shade

Height: 3–5 ft.

Interest: Impressive large leaves that turn red in fall; pink flowers before the foliage appears

This highly ornamental foliage plant is not for the faint-hearted! Umbrella plant (also known as *Darmera*) is a Pacific Coast native with enormous leaves up to 18 inches across, on stalks that can reach 5 feet. It requires lots of space to grow and, in wet spots beside a stream, pond, or bog, it develops into a jungle that delights children. The leaves, which are edged in pointed scallops, are impressive in huge flower arrangements—they turn brilliant red in fall, another plus for this grand plant. The clusters of starry pink flowers show up on 3- to 5-foot stems before the foliage emerges.

HOW TO GROW

Although it prefers to grow in wet, mucky soil, umbrella plant will grow in part shade in humus-rich soil that doesn't dry out. In full sun, it must have its feet in soil that is constantly wet—beside running or standing water. Water the plants well during drought conditions to keep them looking fresh. To propagate, use a pneumatic drill or excavator to chop off pieces of root after the frost has blackened the leaves in fall.

WHERE TO GROW

If you are fortunate enough to have a stream, pond, or bog, grow umbrella plant in the adjacent wet soil. If not, place it in humus-rich, organic soil in a low spot where water collects after rain. It makes a noble sight when allowed to develop into large groups under tall trees.

Top Choices

- *P. peltatum* 'Nana' is a dwarf form that only grows 12 to 15 inches tall, but it is hard to locate in the United States.

- *Petasites japonicus,* var. *giganteus,* giant butterbur, is an unrelated, rugged plant. Its rounded 2-foot leaves and 4- to 6-foot height put it on a similar scale to umbrella plant. It likes the same conditions, but give it lots of room since it spreads vigorously.

GROWING BOG-LOVING PLANTS IN DRY SOIL

Create your own "bog" the easy way with a plastic wading pool. If you don't want a round shape, you can also buy a prefabricated pond liner in the shape you want, but these are more expensive. The larger the wading pool (or pond liner), the better.

1 Lay your "bog liner" in the desired spot and trace its outline on the soil. Dig out soil to match the depth of the liner.

2 Place the plastic liner in the hole and add or remove soil as needed until it is level and its rim is flush with the surrounding ground.

3 Mound some of the removed soil around the edge until the rim is completely buried.

4 Fill with a mix of half soil and half peat moss. Saturate with water and allow it to sit for a few hours before planting to be sure the peat moss has become thoroughly saturated.

5 Fill with perennials such as umbrella plant that like wet soil. Keep your bog well watered, especially during dry spells.

WILD BLUE PHLOX
Phlox divaricata

Zones: 3–9

Bloom Time: Spring

Light: Part shade

Height: 12–15 in.

Interest: Charming, fragrant, blue flowers

Wild blue phlox grows naturally from Quebec to Georgia, showing great adaptability to diverse climates. Its flower color varies from very pale blue to deep sky blue, with occasional purplish blue and pure white variations. The clusters of lightly fragrant flowers sit atop 12- to 15-inch stems of dark green foliage. The plant spreads slowly, but seeds itself to naturally increase the size of the planting. The offspring are frequently a different shade than the parent plant. Wild blue phlox makes itself at home in woodland gardens and spreads to shady locations with conditions it finds comfortable.

HOW TO GROW
Provide wild blue phlox with slightly acidic, humus-rich soil that stays moist but well drained. After flowering and after the seeds have fallen (about four weeks after

the blooms have ended), shear the plants to encourage new leaf growth. No other care is required. Divide established clumps if you wish to start new patches beyond the reach of self-sowing.

WHERE TO GROW

Grow wild blue phlox in woodland gardens, especially along paths, with other spring-flowering wildflowers. It works well as a mild-mannered flowering ground cover, because it will not overrun its neighbors. Give it room to spread itself around and it will produce delightful color combinations, popping up in the most unexpected places—even in mulched paths. Plant extra for cutting—you'll love it in a vase.

Top Choices

- *P.* 'Chattahoochie' is a natural hybrid variety that has lavender-blue flowers with a maroon eye on 10-inch plants.

- *P. divaricata* 'Dirigo Ice' is an exquisite ice blue selection on plants that grow 8 to 12 inches tall.

- *P. divaricata* subsp. *laphamii* has the deepest blue flowers, which appear on 15-inch plants.

- *P.* 'Fuller's White' is stunning pure white and covers itself with blossoms with deeply notched petals on 8- to 12-inch stems.

- *P. glaberrima*, smooth phlox, is a Southeast native and has rose-pink blossoms on 18- to 24-inch plants.

Garden Companions

Mats of wild blue phlox look quite at home with other flowering plants in shaded beds and borders. The phlox makes a good partner for early bloomers in spring and often continues flowering until early summer.

- BLOODROOT
- CRESTED IRIS
- EPIMEDIUM
- FOAMFLOWER
- HOSTA
- JACOB'S-LADDER
- LADY'S-MANTLE
- SIBERIAN BUGLOSS
- SWEET WOODRUFF
- VIRGINIA BLUEBELLS

ON THE SHORT SIDE

Creeping phlox (*P. stolonifera*) likes the same growing conditions as wild blue phlox. In midspring it is covered with lilac blooms. Varieties (all 6 to 10 inches tall and hardy in Zones 2 to 8) include:

- *P.* 'Blue Ridge' (lilac-blue)
- *P.* 'Bruce's White' (white)
- *P.* 'Home Fires' (rich pink)
- *P.* 'Pink Ridge' (mauve)

MAYAPPLE
Podophyllum peltatum

Zones: 3–9

Bloom Time: Spring to early summer

Light: Part shade

Height: 15–18 in.

Interest: Handsome native plant with large leaves, white flowers, and edible yellow fruits

Mayapple is native to the woods of eastern and southern North America and provides a different look in ground covers for shade. When young, the plants develop only one large (1 foot across), shiny green, umbrella-like leaf. As it matures, mayapple develops a pair of large leaves on a 15- to 18-inch stem. Its nodding, 2-inch-wide, solitary white blossom appears at the fork between the two leaves. Later, the plant develops a large, yellow, egg-shaped, edible fruit that can be used to make jams and jellies. Unless you're looking for them, it's easy to miss the flowers and fruits of mayapple since they're tucked away under the pair of leaves. Mayapple's underground shoots ramble to form large colonies—so give it lots of room.

CAUTION: *Although the leaves and roots have medicinal properties, they are very poisonous if eaten in large quantities.*

HOW TO GROW

Mayapple prefers rich, moist, organic soil. On sites that do not offer evenly moist soil, it needs to be mulched heavily with leaf compost or chopped leaves and watered in dry weather. Otherwise, this plant is maintenance-free. Create new plantings by digging up pieces of the plant as it goes dormant and transplanting to the desired new location.

WHERE TO GROW

Mayapple is a woodland wildflower and grows best in sites that mimic its natural home. The ideal location for mayapple is on a moist bank or a raised knoll in the woodland garden so that the nodding white flowers and yellow fruits can be seen more easily. Use it as a ground cover under tall trees or beside large shrubs, and interplant it with other vigorous growers to create a tapestry of textures. In the far North, it will grow in full sun if the soil remains constantly moist but not waterlogged.

Top Choice

- *P. hexandrum,* Himalayan mayapple, has rosy white, upward-facing flowers, large purplish brown mottled leaves, and red fruits. It is less hardy than the native species. Zones 6 to 9.

MYSTERIOUS MANDRAKE

Mayapple is also called American mandrake in reference to its resemblance to that powerful herb.

Mandrake is native to southeastern Europe and has large, pointed leaves and small whitish flowers. The small, round, yellow fruits have a floral odor. The most powerful part of the mandrake plant is believed to be the forked roots, which have a vaguely human shape.

Mandrake has been used for everything from inducing a deathlike coma in crucifixion victims to freeing those suffering from demonic possession.

American mandrake is not closely related to mandrake, but it has nevertheless developed a reputation just as mysterious.

Native Americans used mayapple in remedies meant to stimulate the liver and intestines. (All parts except the fruits are very poisonous, however.) The herb was regarded as very powerful medicine by shamans of many nations. Some sources say that mayapple was even used by those wishing to commit suicide. Today an extract from mayapple is used as an anti-cancer medicine.

Jacob's-Ladder
Polemonium caeruleum

Zones: 3–9

Bloom Time: Late spring to early summer

Light: Part shade

Height: 18–24 in.

Interest: Airy spikes of bright blue or white flowers and attractive fernlike foliage

Jacob's-ladder is a European native whose colloquial name originated from the leaves that resemble the ladder in Jacob's dream in the book of Genesis 28:12. It is a free-flowering perennial that blooms in late spring and early summer with 1-inch blue or white blossoms on upright stems. The bright green, fernlike foliage remains attractive after the plant has flowered. It has an American cousin, creeping Jacob's-ladder (*P. reptans*), which is longer lived in the garden than its European counterpart; its spreading 8- to 15-inch stems produce masses of twinkling lavender-blue flowers.

How to Grow

Jacob's-ladder tends to be a short-lived perennial, but it usually self-sows to replace itself. It needs only average garden or woodsy soil that doesn't get too dry or too wet. Remove the flower spikes after the seedpods have turned brown. To ensure replacement plants, shake pods around the original plant or in new areas to scatter the seeds. Watch out for seedlings the following spring; they quickly develop the characteristic laddered foliage. Thin the seedlings so they don't crowd out each other.

WHERE TO GROW

Jacob's-ladder is useful in any woodland setting as well as in a mixed border. So that the entire plant may be seen and appreciated to its fullest, don't crowd it with other plants. It is ideal planted with shorter-growing plants so that the Jacob's-ladder flower spikes stand well above its neighbors. It may not thrive in really hot summers.

Top Choices

- *P.* 'Album' has pure white flowers.

- *P.* 'Apricot Delight' gets its name from the apricot-yellow centers of its lilac-blue flowers.

- *P.* 'Brise d'Anjou' has lilac-blue flowers above dramatic, cream-variegated leaves. Zones 4 to 7.

- *P. reptans,* creeping Jacob's-ladder, is an eastern American native with sparkling. lavender-blue, springtime flowers on 8- to 15-inch plants. 'Firmament' is an improved selection with bright blue flowers on 20-inch stems.

MAKING MORE JACOB'S-LADDER

Even though Jacob's-ladder is very good at self-sowing, it doesn't hurt to lend a helping hand. By assisting nature you can also increase your garden's bounty of this beautiful perennial.

In summer allow the flowers to fade. They will be replaced with small, brown, three-celled seed capsules. In early autumn collect the seeds from the capsules as they break open. Lightly cultivate the area beneath the parent plant, removing any plant debris and leaving a smooth bed of soil. Sprinkle the seeds onto the soil and gently pat them into the ground with your palm. Lay a very thin coating of vermiculite over the seeds and moisten with a fine spray of water. If all goes well, seedlings of Jacob's-ladder will appear in early to midspring.

VARIEGATED SOLOMON'S-SEAL

Polygonatum odoratum 'Variegatum'

Zones: 4–9

Bloom Time: Spring and early summer

Light: Part shade

Height: 18–24 in.

Interest: Arching stems with fragrant white flowers and attractive white-variegated foliage

The showy leaves of variegated Solomon's-seal are bright green, edged in white. This coloration makes a shady spot positively sparkle all season long. Like other Solomon's-seals, this variety has graceful, arching, unbranched stems; pairs of 1-inch white flowers hang down from the axils of the leaves. The flowers have a fragrance that is particularly delightful on warm, calm evenings.

HOW TO GROW

Variegated Solomon's-seal requires a rich, woodsy soil; while it tolerates dryness, it grows best in soil that stays relatively moist, but never waterlogged. Incorporate lots of leaf compost, peat moss, or other organic matter before planting. After planting, keep the soil mulched to conserve moisture and suppress weeds. Water plantings during dry spells. To start new plants, dig up portions of the plants with a sharp spade in fall, after the foliage has been touched by frost. Alternatively, mark the location of plants in fall and transplant in spring before they break dormancy and poke above the ground.

WHERE TO GROW

This plant is attractive and useful for adding elegance to shady locales—especially when planted amid a ground cover such as hosta, pachysandra, or periwinkle. Its elegant, arching stems provide a very pleasing contrast to the lower-growing plants. Touches of white on the leaves provide the added dimension of color contrast in a swath of shady greens. Plant some near a path so that its sweet fragrance can be readily enjoyed.

Top Choices

- *P. commutatum,* great Solomon's-seal, is a large and impressive American native whose arching stems reach 3 to 5 feet (and sometimes even taller!). It really makes a statement in the shade garden. Unusual, yellowish green and white flowers are followed by round, dark navy blue fruits. It spreads, so give it lots of room to grow.

- *P. falcatum,* dwarf Japanese Solomon's-seal, grows only 8 to 10 inches tall. *P. humile* is another, similar dwarf Asian species; the two are often interchanged in nurseries, but both are delightful plants so it makes little difference. Zones 4 to 8.

Garden Companions

Plant Solomon's-seal in clumps out of arm's reach behind any of the perennials listed below so children won't be tempted by their black, berrylike fruits. Though not a serious threat, they will cause an upset stomach if ingested.

- BLUE-EYED MARY
- HOSTA
- JAPANESE PRIMROSE
- LILY-OF-THE-VALLEY
- MAYAPPLE
- PERIWINKLE
- SELF-HEAL
- SWEET WOODRUFF
- UPRIGHT BUGLE

SOLOMON'S GLUE?

It is said that a sixteenth-century Englishman noted the various joints on *Polygonatum* stems and the leaf-stalk scars left on rhizomes at season's end. He reasoned in the fashion of his age that if the roots were pulverized and drunk with ale, they would "gleweth together the bones," sealing broken bones and open wounds; hence the name Solomon's-seal.

JAPANESE PRIMROSE
Primula japonica

Zones: 5–8

Bloom Time: Late spring to early summer

Light: Part shade

Height: 18–24 in.

Interest: Showy whorls of colorful flowers for several weeks

The Japanese primrose is one of the easiest-to-grow members of this large, but sometimes fussy, genus. It produces beautiful, colorful flowers. In the moist to wet conditions that it prefers, the Japanese primrose will grow into a vigorous clump with several 18- to 24-inch flower stems. Its characteristic whorls of flowers are tiered like candelabras and appear in shades of carmine or crimson red, pink, and white. The plants cross-pollinate freely to produce seedlings of intermediate shades—with dark red being the dominant hue.

HOW TO GROW
This colorful plant must have rich, slightly acidic, moist to wet soil that never dries out. Japanese primrose will even grow in running water that completely covers the plant for short periods. It self-sows freely to produce

dense groups. It can be grown in ordinary woodland conditions but it must be well watered during any drought. Buy nursery starts or plant from seeds.

WHERE TO GROW

If given room, this primrose naturalizes readily to form large clumps. Japanese primrose loves wet feet, so choose a home for it in any area that stays moist or wet. Good locations include beside or in shallow water, a stream, bog, pond, or just a low spot where water regularly collects after rain. In northern climates, it will grow in full sun if the soil is constantly wet. If there is a damp or wet spot in your garden, don't deprive yourself of this colorful display.

Top Choices

- *P. auricula,* auricula, is an extraordinary primrose that has been hybridized to produce some of the most colorful plants. It has thick, fleshy leaves, and the clustered flowers in every shade except true blue appear on 8-inch stems. Zones 3 to 7.

- *P. denticulata,* drumstick primrose, has a round flower head of fragrant pink, lilac, red, or white flowers on 8- to 10-inch stems. Flowers last for several weeks in early spring. Zones 3 to 8.

- *P. veris,* cowslip, has nodding, pale yellow blossoms on 6- to 8-inch stems. Zones 4 to 8.

PRIMROSE PLANTINGS

Because the dark red selections of Japanese primrose are more vigorous, they soon dominate a planting. To produce a softer, more ethereal display, dig out the darker shades as soon as young plants show their color. Transplant these to another location, or pass them on to friends to start their own colony. A fine example of this refinement is the garden of Chanticleer in Wayne, Pennsylvania.

KEEPING SNAILS AND SLUGS OUT

You can protect small plantings, raised beds, and containers from slugs or snails by installing copper barriers. Rolls of very thin copper strips are available from garden centers and supply catalogs. Install these along the edge of containers or planters, or around small plantings. Slugs and snails can't crawl across copper. Wear gloves when handling the copper strips, because the edges are razor sharp.

POLYANTHA PRIMROSE
Primula x *polyantha*

Zones: 5–8

Bloom Time: Early to late spring

Light: Filtered shade

Height: 6–12 in.

Interest: Multicolored blossoms with contrasting yellow eyes; easy to grow in moist, semishaded locations

Polyantha primroses are a popular group of hybrids that have evolved from repeated crossings of several genera, including *P. elatior*, *P. juliae*, and *P. vulgaris* (the English primrose). They form tight, low clumps of crinkled and deeply veined leaves; many are evergreen but others die back in winter. All are glorious in full bloom, lighting up shadowy areas with their cheery flower clusters in radiant colors. Few other plants embody the essence of spring with the verve and gaiety of the polyantha primrose.

HOW TO GROW
Plant primroses in rich, slightly acidic soil, fortified with plenty of organic matter and kept moist during the spring growth spurt and bloom periods. Though they'll survive with less water in summer and fall, polyantha primroses

do best in moist soil. You can help keep the ground moist and cool by mulching well with compost or another organic material. Divide crowded clumps after flowering in spring or in early autumn. If you notice snail or slug damage, go out on an early-morning foray and pluck off these munching pests. (Also see pages 35 and 89.)

WHERE TO GROW

The polyanthas are perfect primroses for beds in semi-shaded lawns, glorious either in formal masses or in small colonies. They tuck easily into rock gardens and are ideal in wide, shallow pots on covered patios and decks. The polyanthas are excellent edging plants along perennial borders in part sun, bursting into flower while late bloomers are just getting started with spring growth. When background plants mature later in the season, they shield the primroses from harsh summer sun.

Top Choices

- Cowichan Series hybrids have bronze-toned, dark green foliage. Solid-colored flowers (red, blue, maroon, purple, or yellow) have a velvety feel.

- Crescendo Series cultivars are the earliest-blooming polyanthas. Their brilliant flowers in nearly every color have yellow centers and are carried in large clusters on 8- to 10-inch stems.

- Rainbow Series polyanthas have shorter-stemmed blooms with yellow centers. Colors range from blue, carmine, scarlet, and pink to white, yellow, and cream.

PLANTING A PRIMROSE PATH

Though it may sound like a description from a romantic tale, a primrose-lined path makes as welcome an entry to a brick home as it does to an English cottage garden.

1 After the last frost in spring, dig a trench 6 inches deep about 1 foot away from a path or sidewalk. If your soil is poor, amend the planting area with several inches of compost dug into the bed. Work in the recommended amount of a slow-release, low-nitrogen fertilizer.

2 Place primroses 8 to 12 inches apart, loosening their roots with your fingers as you set them in the trench. Gently firm the soil around them so they sit at the same level as they did in their nursery containers.

3 Water your plants well and cover the soil with 1 to 2 inches of mulch. Small wood chips, compost, or pine needles look nice under the foliage rosettes. Continue to keep the soil moist during dry spells.

SELF-HEAL
Prunella grandiflora

Zones: 5–10

Bloom Time: Summer

Light: Part shade

Height: 10–12 in.

Interest: Colorful, easy-to-grow ground cover

Self-heal is an unassuming, low-growing, undemanding plant with colorful summer flowers. The species has showy, hooded, purple blossoms that sit above leaves on 10- to 12-inch stems. Named selections have been developed for larger flowers and come in blue, lilac, pink, red, or white. When planted in sweeps, self-heal makes a colorful tapestry. The common name originated from the medicinal properties that this plant was said to possess.

CAUTION: *Avoid the common* P. vulgaris, *because it is an unimpressive, weedy species.*

HOW TO GROW
Self-heal prefers a shady site but will grow in full sun in cool climates. While it tolerates ordinary soil, it does best in soil that is rich in organic matter and evenly

moist, but never waterlogged. To maintain a tidy appearance, deadhead after the flowers have faded. To increase the size of your plantings, divide the crowns (pull them apart) and transplant to new areas. Do this in early spring before the flower spikes start to show, or in late summer. Dig up and relocate (or give away) any plants that spread beyond where they're wanted.

WHERE TO GROW

Self-heal makes an ideal ground cover for the front of a shady border or alongside a woodland path. It's also useful and attractive in containers such as window boxes or patio planters. Underplant self-heal with spring-flowering bulbs such as Siberian squill or small varieties of daffodils to provide early color before it starts to bloom.

Top Choices

- *P.* 'Pink Loveliness' has large, bright pink blossoms.

- *P.* 'Purple Loveliness' has white highlights on its deep purple flowers.

- *P.* 'White Loveliness' has white blossoms.

WHAT'S IN A NAME?

Gardening is a pastime that nearly everyone can enjoy. Yet if there is one aspect of this pleasant vocation that is difficult for many to warm to, it is fumbling with a plant's scientific name.

To most of us the strange-sounding Latin names of plants mean nothing, but many times they tell a story about the plant's distant past. Such is the case with self-heal.

The generic name of self-heal, also called heal-all, is *Prunella.* It acquired this name in the sixteenth century during an epidemic in Germany in which many people became ill with a mysterious disease whose dominant symptom was a brown discoloration of the tongue. Because of this, the sickness was called "browns."

Many treatments were tried but only one, an herb with a blunt flower head filled with bluish blossoms, actually seemed to cure the browns. Because of this, the plant was given the name brunella (brown), which over time became *Prunella.*

Knowing the stories behind some of the garden plants we grow can make the experience of caring for them even more rewarding.

SPOTTED LUNGWORT

Pulmonaria saccharata

Zones: 3–9

Bloom Time: Spring

Light: Part shade

Height: 10–12 in.

Interest: Colorful flowers followed by ornamental, spotted foliage that remains attractive all summer long

Spotted lungwort provides two seasons of interest. It starts in spring with pink, blue, or white, trumpet-shaped flowers on 10- to 12-inch stems. These are followed by showy green foliage that is spotted silver-gray; in some newer selections, the entire leaf may be silver-gray. The pink- and blue-flowered varieties often open as one color (pink) and turn to the other (blue) as they mature. Lungwort is so named because its leaves are said to look like a diseased lung.

HOW TO GROW

Spotted lungwort will grow in ordinary soil. For the foliage to remain good looking all summer, it must be grown in a shady location in rich, organic soil that never dries out, yet never stays too wet. Some varieties are susceptible to powdery mildew; this fungal disease is more noticeable on plants that have been stressed from growing in conditions that are too wet or too dry. To increase the size of your planting, divide the crowns carefully as soon as the flowers are past their peak. Plant divisions in good rich soil and water thoroughly as the new leaves emerge.

WHERE TO GROW

Plant spotted lungwort under the high shade of tall trees or large shrubs. It looks most at home when interplanted with native wildflowers and spring-flowering bulbs. Lungwort's showy foliage provides a long season of interest when planted alongside ground covers such as pachysandra that are solid green, or those that flower in early spring and are green for the rest of the year, such as periwinkle.

Top Choices

- *P.* 'Mrs. Moon' has flowers that are pink when they first open and turn lilac and then blue. Leaves are deep green with silver spots. The leaves of 'British Sterling' are white with green edges; flower buds are magenta opening to blue. 'Sissinghurst White' is a white-flowered version.

- *P. angustifolia* has brilliant blue flowers set off with dark green foliage. 'Azurea' is an early-blooming selection with even brighter blue flowers.

- *P. longifolia,* longleaf lungwort, has narrower leaves and tolerates hot, humid summers better. 'Bertram Anderson' and 'Roy Davidson' are good selections with showier flowers.

SUMMER SPRUCE-UP

During early to midsummer, ornamental plant foliage often looks the worse for wear because of slug or snail damage, stress from disease (such as powdery mildew), or damage from hail or thunderstorms. Freshen the garden by cutting away some of the spoiled leaves and spent flowers. Plants such as lady's-mantle, Siberian bugloss, umbrella plant, hosta, lungwort, and rodgersia all benefit from this summer cleanup.

THE DOCTRINE OF SIGNATURES

Lungwort's name refers to its past reputation as a cure for lung diseases (now of questionable validity).

Its use as a pulmonary cure came from the likeness of its randomly splotched leaves to diseased lung tissue, a connection that followed the Doctrine of Signatures. This doctrine espoused that the way a plant looked determined which parts of the body it could heal.

FEATHERLEAF RODGERSIA

Rodgersia pinnata

Zones: 5–9

Bloom Time: Late spring to early summer

Light: Part shade

Height: 36–48 in.

Interest: Showy rose-red flowers and large, attractive, bronze leaves

Featherleaf rodgersia produces lovely plumes of 3- to 4-foot, rose-red, well-branched flower spikes with a multitude of tiny flowers that together produce lots of color. These are set off by very beautiful bronze foliage that is similar to a horse chestnut leaf, with its broad leaflets arranged like the fingers of a hand. This plant is a large, shade-loving perennial from the Orient that provides a flourish of color in late spring and early summer. Its highly ornamental foliage provides a distinctive accent to the woodland or formal shady garden for the remainder of the growing season.

HOW TO GROW

Featherleaf rodgersia requires humus-rich soil that remains constantly moist, but it does not like standing water. It resents drying out, which will cause leaves (or leaf edges) to turn brown. To promote even soil moisture, mulch heavily and water thoroughly during dry spells. In northern climates, it will tolerate full sun if grown in damp soil near a stream, pond, or bog; it appreciates winter protection wherever snow cover is unreliable. Featherleaf rodgersia will survive in many parts of Zone 4 if given winter protection.

WHERE TO GROW

This plant looks best when featured as an accent plant amid one or more low-growing ground covers in a shade border or woodland garden. Even when not in bloom, its big leaves add architectural interest to any planting. It can also be used in combination with other bold-leafed plants such as umbrella plant, large-leafed hostas, bigleaf goldenray, giant butterbur, and tall ferns. This produces a feeling of the Tropics in a temperate climate.

Top Choices

- R. *aesculifolia*, fingerleaf rodgersia, features large 3- to 6-foot plumes of creamy white summer blossoms above large green leaves with tints of bronze; bristly leaf stems are rust colored.

- R. *podophylla*, bronzeleaf rodgersia, is similar to fingerleaf rodgerisia, but its oversized, maplelike foliage is shiny green and turns bronze in summer.

RODGERSIA AND WATER

The large, dynamic foliage of any rodgersia is definitely a bold addition to the garden. The challenge is to find a place for it and other bold plants where they don't overpower their neighbors. A convenient solution can be found in water.

Rodgersia thrives in the moist soils near ponds and streams. A planting nestled near the edge of water reflects the foliage and softens the dramatic texture of its foliage.

A nice aspect of rodgersia's bold personality is that a little goes a long way. Just two or three plants set near water will provide a beautiful display.

IN HONOR OF RODGERS

Rodgersia is native to regions of eastern Asia, including China and Japan. Many years ago an expedition lead by Admiral John Rodgers went to Asia, where the expedition scientists discovered this plant. The plant was named rodgersia in honor of the officer in command.

BLOODROOT
Sanguinaria canadensis

Zones: 3–9

Bloom Time: Early spring

Light: Part shade

Height: 4–8 in.

Interest: Starry white flowers and beautiful gray-green leaves that form a pleasing ground cover

Bloodroot is one of the joys of spring in the woods of eastern North America. It emerges from the ground with leaves wrapped around the bud; the leaves unroll as the flowers open. The 2-inch-wide, purest white blossoms open early, with the flowers each having eight or more petals. Sadly, they remain open but a few days. The lovely blooms are followed by highly distinctive gray-green, lobed foliage that remains attractive for most of the summer, making an interesting and unusual ground cover. Both scientific and common names are derived from the bloodred sap that is produced by the thick, fleshy rhizomes. It was used by some Native Americans as a dye for clothing and as body paint.

CAUTION: Bloodroot rhizomes are toxic—don't eat them!

HOW TO GROW

Choose a spot with part shade and rich, woodsy soil that retains moisture, but is well drained. Place the thick bloodroot rhizomes horizontally and 1 inch deep in soil. Add lots of organic matter before planting. Mulch annually with chopped leaves or compost in fall after the foliage has died down. Water thoroughly in dry conditions to prevent the foliage from going dormant and disappearing. Divide the rhizomes in late summer when the leaves turn yellow. Bloodroot spreads both by the rhizomes and from self-sown seedlings to form a moderately large colony.

WHERE TO GROW

Many agree that no woodland garden is complete without a large patch of bloodroot. Plant it toward the front of a formal shade garden for spring and summer beauty. Or sprinkle plants along the edge of a path in a shady bower. Use it for a ground cover under deciduous shrubs; mix several patches among other not-too-aggressive ground covers (such as Allegheny spurge or European ginger) to cover large areas beneath deciduous trees.

Top Choice

• S. 'Multiplex', double bloodroot, produces one of the most beautiful blossoms of all—one that looks like a pure white water lily blossom.

PLANTING
BLOODROOT

It has become garden lore that plants regarded as wildflowers, such as bloodroot, are difficult to grow. They are actually easy to grow; at planting time, take the time to site them well, prepare the soil, and plant them correctly. Once established they will reward you each spring with their delicate blossoms and interesting foliage for little added effort.

1 In fall prepare the soil by cultivating with a garden fork or similar tool to a depth of 8 to 10 inches.

2 Mix in good amounts of compost or another form of organic matter so the soil looks dark and rich.

3 Dig holes in the prepared soil approximately 5 inches long, 3 inches wide, and 4 inches deep.

4 Hold the rhizome horizontally about 1 inch below the soil surface and backfill the hole beneath the rhizome.

5 Firm the soil around the rhizome and water in well.

FALSE SOLOMON'S-SEAL
Smilacina racemosa

Zones: 3–9

Bloom Time: Spring to early summer

Light: Part shade

Height: 24–36 in.

Interest: Elegant, arching stems with bright green foliage and fragrant, creamy white flowers at the tips

False Solomon's-seal is native to North America and has found its way into many woodland gardens across the country. In spring and early summer, each 2- to 3-foot stem is tipped with a plumelike cluster of fragrant, starlike, creamy white flowers. These are followed by green berries that ripen to a speckled pinkish red. The unbranched stems arch gracefully and have wide, bright green leaves arrayed along the sides. The foliage remains ornamental all summer long. Plants spread slowly to produce handsome groups; it must know it looks its best in large patches.

HOW TO GROW

As with other native woodland plants, false Solomon's-seal is happiest in light shade and slightly acidic soil that's rich in organic matter. However, it isn't too fussy as long as the soil remains somewhat moist (not wet) during the growing season. It tolerates competition from surface tree roots better than many shade plants. The best time to divide and transplant is when the plants go dormant in late summer. New plants can also be produced from seeds collected from the ripe fruits in late summer.

WHERE TO GROW

False Solomon's-seal blends well with, hosta, rodgersia, globeflower, and native wildflowers such as ladybells. Use it to add a graceful note to a massed planting of low ground covers, or in groups to replace lawn around tree trunks. To enjoy its sweet fragrance, plant near an often-used path.

Top Choices

- *S. stellata,* starflower Solomon's-seal, is also native to the eastern United States. It is similar to false Solomon's-seal, but the flowers are more starlike, the berries are larger, and the 1- to 2-foot stems grow more erect.

- *S. trifolia,* is a charming wildflower that is at home in wet places. It makes a perfect plant for the bog garden or streamside planting.

Garden Companions

Intermingle groupings of three to five false Solomon's-seal with any of the plants listed here. The tall, arching stems add structure and height to beds and borders.

- BLEEDING-HEART
- FERNS
- GLOBEFLOWER
- HOSTA
- JACK-IN-THE-PULPIT
- JAPANESE PRIMROSE
- LADYBELLS
- MAYAPPLE
- MEADOW-RUE
- RODGERSIA
- WILD BLUE PHLOX

SELECTING A
HEALTHY PLANT

Good-looking gardens start with healthy plants. When you purchase new plants, avoid those with bare stems, discolored leaves, or insect damage. Instead, look for dense, rich green foliage with no broken stems and no injuries from pests or diseases. Be suspicious of large plants in small pots; they are often rootbound and recover slowly after planting.

CELANDINE POPPY
Stylophorum diphyllum

Zones: 4–9

Bloom Time: Spring and early summer

Light: Part shade

Height: 12–18 in.

Interest: Brilliant, butter yellow flowers above attractive blue-green foliage

Celandine poppy, also called wood poppy, is a beautiful native of eastern North America. It produces 3- to 4-inch, butter yellow, upward-facing flowers similar to those of the Welsh poppy. The highly ornamental, deeply lobed, blue-green foliage has a matte surface very similar to bloodroot—the pair make delightful companions. Celandine poppy is a not-too-fussy, low-maintenance plant that self-sows, spreading freely but not invasively to form large colonies. Stems produce a bright orange-yellow sap that was used by Native Americans to make a natural dye.

How to Grow
Celandine poppy is easy to grow in woodsy soil that doesn't dry out. If allowed to dry out in the summer, it will survive, but the foliage will disappear as plants go

dormant. Mulch around the plants and water well during rainless spells. It self-sows freely to produce lots of new plants—if you don't want seedlings, deadhead to prevent this. Little other care is required, and it is relatively pest-free. The plants may be moved to new locations when they are very small, but they are best left undisturbed once established because of their brittle, fleshy roots.

WHERE TO GROW

With the delightful habit of popping up in unexpected places to compose interesting combinations of color, texture and form, celandine poppy is most at home in woodland gardens where it can romp at will. The plants add delightful visual appeal when interplanted with spring-flowering bulbs such as Spanish bluebells, grape hyacinth, and camassia.

A Word of Caution

Don't confuse this plant with another related celandine, *Chelidonium majus*. Though they are related and the leaves of both look quite similar, this celandine has a much smaller flower and a problematic, weedy disposition.

Garden Companions

Plant celandine poppies for bright, sunny yellow polka dots scattered throughout the dissected green foliage. They stand out sharply among woodland favorites such as those listed below:

- BLEEDING-HEART
- BLOODROOT
- JACOB'S-LADDER
- LADYBELLS
- LENTEN ROSE
- SIBERIAN BUGLOSS
- SPANISH BLUEBELLS
- UPRIGHT BUGLE
- VIRGINIA BLUEBELLS
- WILD BLUE PHLOX

ANNUALS FOR SHADE

Summer annuals are invaluable as fillers for bare problem spots in perennial gardens. For color along border edges in lightly filtered shade, plant waxleaf begonias and violas; place taller forget-me-nots and flowering tobacco in the middle of beds. Where shade is heavier, choose impatiens or monkey flower for summer blossoms, or opt for the bright foliage patterns of coleus and caladium.

MEADOW RUE
Thalictrum

Zones: 4–9

Bloom Time: Late summer to early fall

Light: Part shade to full sun

Height: 6–8 ft.

Interest: Very tall and incredibly elegant stems with beautiful blue-green foliage; topped with a mist of lavender flowers

Meadow rue is a sensational perennial, a tall plant that is remarkably delicate and graceful in appearance. The cultivar 'Lavender Mist' is unique in the world of hardy perennials because of its imposing height; nevertheless, it manages to be amazingly graceful. The summer-to-fall visual feast begins with lacy, columbine-like, blue-green foliage that appears on windproof purple stems. This is followed by a cloud of lavender to purple blossoms that appear in a large, well-branched spray above the towering stems.

HOW TO GROW

In the North, meadow rue can be grown in full sun, providing the soil is rich, well-drained loam that stays evenly moist. In the South, it requires the same soil conditions but can only be grown in part shade. (It does not handle the dry heat of the Southwest very well.) Once established, the very strong, thick-stemmed plants rarely need staking and should be left undisturbed. Divide plants in spring only to increase your supply. They are surprisingly narrow (and delicate) for their height; plants should be spaced only 18 inches apart for the best effect.

WHERE TO GROW

Meadow rue is a choice plant that can stand on its own in large beds. It is more commonly mixed in with other plants to act as a towering accent above its neighbors. It's an obvious back-of-the-border plant, but try it in the middle of a border, too, for the plants behind it can still be seen through its delicate floral display.

Top Choices

- *T. aquilegifolium,* columbine meadow rue, produces masses of blossoms in fluffy tufts atop 3- to 4-foot stems. It is the best species for the climate of the Southeast. Zones 5 to 10.

- *T. delavayi,* Yunnan meadow rue, is a shorter, early-summer-flowering plant. 'Hewitt's Double' is double flowered and much desired because its floral display is longer lasting than its single-flowered cousins.

- *T.* 'Lavender Mist' is a stately plant reaching 8 feet tall. The soft-textured, blue-green leaves are attractive throughout the growing season. In mid- to late-summer, graceful flower stems dotted with lavender blossoms rise above the foliage—a nice diversion from the profusion of summer reds and yellows.

RAISED BEDS FOR WET PLACES

If you have poorly drained soil that sprouts puddles better than plants, you can still enjoy a planting of perennials with little effort.

Where soils are not well drained, consider planting in raised beds instead. Construct a raised bed atop your poorly drained area. It can be made of landscape timbers, stone, or even framed 2 x 12 planking.

Once built, fill the bed with soil blended with compost or another type of organic matter at a rate of about 1:1. Mix in a dusting of slow-release fertilizer and some sand if it's handy, stir well, and spread evenly throughout the bed. Then plant your perennials. See page 45 for how to maintain the rich soil in your raised bed.

FOAMFLOWER

Tiarella cordifolia

Zones: 3–9

Bloom Time: Spring

Light: Part to full shade

Height: 6–12 in.

Interest: Masses of frothy white flowers, tinged in pink; attractive, pale green foliage with burgundy veins; a tough ground cover

Foamflower is a pretty ground cover whose starry white flowers have a noticeable pink blush—especially apparent as the blossoms age. The pale green, evergreen foliage is delightfully veined with burgundy; in winter and when grown in only part shade, the entire leaf usually turns bronze-burgundy. This easy-to-grow, spreading species carpets the ground with a dense mat and grows well at the base of shrubs and other tall plants. Foamflower adapts well to diverse areas and sites. In recent years, new, larger selections have been developed with highly ornamental foliage.

HOW TO GROW

Foamflower is a tough little plant; it isn't bothered by pests and requires little care to keep it growing and flowering. Like most other native woodland species, foamflower is happiest in rich, organic soil that never dries out and never stays soggy. Before planting, incorporate lots of organic matter into the soil; also mulch with compost or chopped leaves every year in late fall or early spring to maintain a high humus level. Dig up and divide the plants in early spring before they begin flowering or in the early summer after flowering. (Water well afterward and shade with newspaper.) You can also divide foamflower in fall.

WHERE TO GROW

Grow foamflower as a delicately textured ground cover in shady sites under trees, shrubs, or other tall perennials. It blends well with most plants and looks especially attractive with spring-flowering bulbs poking through its mat. It is particularly useful for covering large areas; in the right conditions it spreads freely and quickly.

Top Choices

- *T. wherryi,* Wherry's foamflower, is very similar to its cousin, but it doesn't run; this clump-forming species is also taller. It's the better bet if your space is limited, because it will never outgrow its area. It is sometimes offered as *T. collina.*

- x *Heucherella,* with its charming, pale pink, wandlike flowers on 18-inch stems, is a hybrid of coralbells (*Heuchera*) and foamflower (*Tiarella*). Zones 5 to 9.

Garden Companions

Foamflower is a "must" for most shade gardens. It blends beautifully with all of the plants listed below:

- ASIATIC LILY
- BLEEDING-HEART
- BLUE-EYED MARY
- DAFFODIL
- HOSTA
- LENTEN ROSE
- PERENNIAL GERANIUMS
- SIBERIAN BUGLOSS
- SELF-HEAL
- SWEET VIOLET
- SWEET WOODRUFF
- WILD BLUE PHLOX
- YELLOW CORYDALIS

WELL-BEHAVED
CLUMPS

T. wherryi is a perfect little clumper for nestling at the base of large stones in a shaded rock garden. The compact tufts will stay put where you plant them, sending up their flowery wands in soft contrast to steely gray or rusty brown rocks. Choose the larger and denser clumping cultivar 'Oakleaf' to balance the scale of large boulders.

TOAD LILY
Tricyrtis hirta

Zones: 5–9

Bloom Time: Late summer to fall

Light: Part shade

Height: 24–36 in.

Interest: Fascinating flowers on plants resembling Solomon's-seal

Despite its unflattering name, toad lily is a charming Oriental plant that flowers late in the year when there isn't much color in the shade garden. The 1-inch blossoms must be seen up close to be fully appreciated. They have six white petals (tepals, technically—see page 57), spotted in purple and maroon. Their six-part stamens protrude from the flower in a very interesting arrangement. Flowers grow in a row like a chain of orchids draped along the stem. With leaves arranged on either side of an unbranched but elegantly arched stem, the foliage resembles that of Solomon's-seal.

HOW TO GROW

Toad lily requires the same conditions as Solomon's-seal and many other shade plants—rich, woodsy soil that never dries out, but never floods. Incorporate lots of leaf compost or peat moss before planting, keep the soil mulched, and water well during drought. Divide plants in early spring before they break dormancy. Don't cut down the leaves in fall; that will make it easy to find them in spring to divide for more plants.

WHERE TO GROW

Grow toad lily in shady areas where color is needed toward the end of the gardening season. It blends in well with other plants, but to enjoy it to its fullest, plant it at the edge of the border or beside a path where the remarkable flowers can easily be seen up close. Plant enough so you can cut a few to bring inside, for these make good (and fascinating) cut flowers. Underplanting with autumn crocus (*Colchicum autumnale*) makes a really striking combination.

Top Choices

- *T.* 'Alba' has greenish white flowers.

- *T.* 'Variegata' and 'Miyazaki Gold' have striking cream-edged leaves and pink to white flowers spotted pale purple and crimson.

- *T.* 'White Towers' has arching 24- to 36-inch stems with pure white flowers.

- *T. formosana*, Formosa toad lily, has 24- to 36-inch branching stems with dark green leaves and white flowers that are heavily spotted with purple. 'Amethystina', with its bluish purple flowers, is a noteworthy selection.

- *T. f. stolonifera* is taller and runs more freely, making it a good ground cover.

SHADY SITES

Within the world of shade gardening, you'll find plants that accept all degrees of shade while others are tolerant only of certain types. Your garden will flourish best when you match your perennials with the kinds of shade that are cast over the planting beds during different seasons.

Relegate your most sun-sensitive plants to areas of deepest shade—beneath heavy tree canopies, on the sunless north side of buildings and fences, or under overhangs where no sun penetrates.

Plants that must have brighter light but no direct sun do well in moderate shade provided by evergreen trees with lower branches removed, or by clumps of deciduous trees, such as those in woodlands. Widely spaced trees with few low branches create part shade. No sun reaches directly underneath at midday, but the open space all around allows morning or afternoon sun to flow beneath their canopies.

Lighter shade is filtered or dappled, and is found beneath uncrowded, open-branched, deciduous trees.

If your perennials will flower more heavily in a bit of sun but cannot tolerate severe intensities, try to plant them in either part or lightly filtered shade. Remove lower tree limbs to let in more indirect light.

HYBRID GLOBEFLOWER
Trollius x *cultorum*

Zones: 4–7

Bloom Time: Late spring to early summer

Light: Part shade to full sun

Height: 24–36 in.

Interest: Globe-shaped flowers in cream, orange, or yellow over large, divided green leaves

Globeflower is an elegant flower for the shade garden. The solitary flowers, shaped like oversized buttercups, sit atop 24- to 36-inch stems. Blossoms of cream, sunny yellow, or rich orange appear in late spring or early summer; some selections produce a second flush of flowers in the late summer or early fall. Its clumps of deeply cleft leaves are attractive all season long. The hybrid forms, indicated by the x in the botanical name, involve several species; all have larger flowers than the wild species. Globeflower is a long-lasting cut flower for spring and early-summer arrangements.

HOW TO GROW

Globeflower grows well in moist to wet soil, as along the edge of a stream, pond, or bog. It also thrives in a border that has heavy loam, rich in organic matter. Take care to keep roots moist; plants will go dormant if allowed to dry out in the summer. However, globeflower resents the humidity and heat of the Deep South. (It does not grow well in the Southwest, either.) Deadheading will prolong the flowering period. Propagate by division in fall, but to increase your plantings it is better to buy new plants, because clumps produce the most spectacular display if they are left undivided.

WHERE TO GROW

Globeflower is suitable for any shade garden. It can be planted with native ferns and wildflowers or mixed with other imported exotics. All shades are pleasing with deep blue flowers such as those of Siberian irises or lupines.

Top Choices

- *T.* x *cultorum* varieties differ in flower color and height. They include 'Alabaster' (cream on sturdy 30-inch stems) and 'Prichard's Giant' (medium yellow-orange on 30- to 40-inch stems).

- *T. chinensis* is often sold as *T. ledebourii*. 'Golden Queen' has tangerine orange flowers on 24-inch stems. It blooms later and tolerates a wider range of conditions than other globeflowers.

- *T. europaeus* 'Superbus' has butter yellow flowers on 20- to 24-inch plants.

Garden Companions

Globeflower looks best planted in masses in the wettest site you have in your garden. It partners well with any of the following perennials and presents a long succession of warm-hued, plump blooms:

- BLUESTAR
- FERNS
- HOSTA
- JAPANESE PRIMROSE
- LADYBELLS
- PEACHLEAF BELLFLOWER
- SPOTTED LUNGWORT
- VARIEGATED SOLOMON'S-SEAL
- WHITE BLEEDING-HEART

BEAUTIFUL BUT
INVASIVE

Several very attractive perennial plants thrive so vigorously in damp, boggy sites that they've become invasive pests, driving out less aggressive natives and other ornamentals. Beware of purple loosestrife (*Lythrum salicaria*), which has become a serious pest in wetlands. In garden situations, comfrey (*Symphytum*) will quickly take over moist, shaded sites, as will the lovely chameleon plant (*Houttuynia*) and knotweed (*Polygonum*).

MERRYBELLS
Uvularia grandiflora

Zones: 3–9

Bloom Time: Spring

Light: Part shade

Height: 12–18 in.

Interest: Charming yellow flowers on a small, graceful plant

This small eastern and central North American native is a sweet plant that never fails to impress—if you take time to notice the flowers. The delicate, bell-shaped, 1- to 1½-inch-long yellow blossoms of merrybells hang down. It is easy to pass them by without a glance because they pull down the tips of the stems. The foliage, resembling a smaller version of Solomon's-seal, remains attractive all season. Merrybells spread with underground shoots but they are noninvasive.

HOW TO GROW
Merrybells prefer rich, well-drained organic soil that stays evenly moist. Therefore, apply mulch in late winter and keep the plants well watered—especially in early summer. Feeding in spring with a balanced fertilizer

encourages more vigorous growth and a better floral display. No other care is required.

WHERE TO GROW

Merrybells flower early with other spring ephemerals and combine well with other native woodland wildflowers and spring-flowering bulbs, such as daffodils and Spanish bluebells. They belong in a woodland garden with other small plants. They also show off well in front of evergreen shrubs such as rhododendron and mountain laurel, where the beautiful blossoms can stand out against dark foliage.

Top Choices

- *U. sessilifolia,* wild oats, is another native that spreads freely but not invasively and has pale yellow flowers on 12-inch plants.

- *Disporum maculatum,* nodding mandarin, is yet another native, similar to merrybells but with speckled white flowers on 24-inch stems. Zones 3 to 8.

FERTILIZING NATIVE WILDFLOWERS

Native wildflowers grow more readily and put on a better display if fertilized in late winter or spring before new shoots emerge. Use a slow-release formula. Organic fertilizers tend to release nutrients more slowly than synthetic fertilizers, which is better for most perennials. Or feed with a balanced liquid fertilizer such as seaweed emulsion while plants are growing.

INVASIVE GROUND COVERS

Ground covers that spread rapidly are invaluable for providing color and greenery or controlling erosion. When they're planted in the wrong location, they may become a nuisance. Before introducing any new plant into your garden, ask your nurseryman about its growth habits. Some aggressive growers can't be reined in at all.

PERIWINKLE
Vinca minor

Zones: 4–9

Bloom Time: Spring

Light: Part to full shade

Height: 6–12 in.

Interest: A great ground cover with sparkling blue or white flowers and evergreen foliage

Periwinkle is a well-known European plant that is extremely useful as a ground cover; it spreads to form dense plantings that remain attractive all year. In spring it provides a galaxy of flowers that are usually a brilliant sky blue, but cultivars also appear in other shades such as violet, purple, or pure white. In summer, the glossy, rich green foliage provides a fresh coolness; in winter, the foliage turns an appealing dark green in contrast to the predominant surrounding shades of gray and brown. Cold temperatures combined with sun can change the color to a more bronzy hue. The flowers provide twinkling spring bouquets for a small vase.

HOW TO GROW
Periwinkle spreads by layering—that is, as the nonflowering shoots spread along the ground they root at the axils

of the leaves. New plants develop from buds in the leaf axils. This habit makes it an excellent ground cover because it is self-propagating and spreads to form thick mats. Periwinkle's use throughout the country in a variety of soils attests to its adaptability. To keep it vigorous, apply a balanced fertilizer around the plantings in late winter and topdress with compost before new growth appears. In rainless periods, water thoroughly to keep it healthy.

WHERE TO GROW

Periwinkle is perfect wherever an evergreen ground cover is needed in shady sites—under large trees or shrubs, to hold banks so they don't erode, or with other ground covers in sweeps to provide a change in textures. It will even grow in full sun in cool climates and moist soil. In areas that get some spring sun, underplant with spring-flowering bulbs.

Top Choices

- *V. minor* selections include 'Alba' (large, pure white flowers on sturdy plants); 'Atropurpurea' (wine-colored flowers on compact plants); 'Aureola' (yellow-variegated leaves and lilac-blue flowers); and 'Bowles' Variety' (large, brilliant lilac-blue flowers).

- *V. major*, large periwinkle, is a large-leafed variety and is hardy in Zones 7 to 10 only. In the North, it is used as a tender perennial in containers such as window boxes and hanging baskets. The species has large blue flowers; the most commonly grown varieties have very showy, variegated foliage.

TENDER PERENNIALS

Tender perennials are those that are not winter hardy in cold climates. Many of the so-called "annuals" used in summer gardens are perennial in frost-free climates. *V. major* is one such plant. Other examples include impatiens, coleus, agapanthus, fuchsia, heliotrope, lantana, pelargonium, and many salvias.

In cold areas, they must be dug up in fall and kept in a pot in a cool greenhouse, conservatory, or basement. The other option is to propagate from cuttings (see page 67). Grow them over winter as small plants for replanting in spring.

OVERWINTERING INDOORS

After you dig up plants from your garden, move them slowly from the cool outdoors to warmer indoor conditions. Plants need several days on a covered patio or porch to acclimate and adjust to lower light levels before they move inside for winter.

TUFTED VIOLET
Viola cornuta

Zones: 5–9

Bloom Time: Summer to fall

Light: Part shade

Height: 8–10 in.

Interest: Masses of small, pansylike flowers from early summer until fall

For sheer abundance of flowers, few perennials come close to producing the number of blossoms (for as long) as the tufted violet. Flowering begins in early summer and continues until hard frost cuts plants down. This plant shrugs off light frosts. Blossoms of tufted violet are 1 to 1½ inches in diameter and often have a light fragrance. Selections are usually of one color and some feature a contrasting eye. They are usually compact growers that spread two to three times as wide as they are tall. Tufted violet is easy to grow and requires little maintenance.

HOW TO GROW
Tufted violet requires evenly moist soil that never dries out and never floods. In these conditions, it will grow in part shade or even in full sun where summers are cool in

the North. In the South, it despairs of the July and August heat and humidity; shear plants back and wait for fall for a second show. Mulch in late winter to retain moisture, but avoid smothering the crowns, which may cause the plants to rot. Deadhead to keep the plants looking fresh and produce more flowers. Tufted violet grows readily from seeds, but it can also be propagated from cuttings.

WHERE TO GROW

Grow large groups of tufted violet wherever you want long-lasting splashes of color. It can be used as a ground cover under trees and shrubs. It also provides summer color amid wildflowers and flowering bulbs that have their spring fling and then take the rest of the year off. This plant is a superb perennial for patio containers and window boxes, because it flowers for such a long period with little care. Pot some up for the kitchen windowsill—they're sure to bring more than a few smiles.

Top Choices

- *V. cornuta* selections are similar to the species in height and form. 'Black Magic' is black, with a yellow eye. 'Chantreyland' is apricot. 'Cutie', a mixture of purple, lavender, and white, is possibly a hybrid with Johnny-jump-up.

- *V. odorata,* sweet violet, has smaller flowers but offers the famous fragrance. It is available in several shades including 'The Czar' (deep violet), 'Rosina' (deep pink), and 'White Czar' (white).

COOL GARDEN COMFORT

Few sights are more beckoning to a garden visitor on a hot, sunny day than a bench in a cool, shaded retreat. A water feature—whether a natural stream, a pond, or a quiet fountain—adds allure to the scene, but filling a garden nook with living bouquets creates a more indelible and irresistible charm.

Bright whites and pale pastels stand out amid deeper green foliage, setting an inviting scene under shade trees. Plant a few low-growing, compact tufts such as primroses, foamflowers, and violets to tickle the feet of your bench. Set taller ladybells, bleeding-hearts, and astilbes around the back, and late-blooming anemones off to the side. Line the paths coming and going with masses of lady's-mantle, mats of maiden pink, and clumps of dwarf hosta.

If too much sun creeps uninvited into your retreat, set up your own portable shade. Use an adjustable umbrella that you can turn by the hour or the season to keep you and your plants cool and comfortable.

GLOSSARY

Accent plant: A plant that draws attention by its extraordinary display.

Acidic soil: Soil with a pH value of less than 7.0.

Alkaline soil: Soil with a pH value of more than 7.0.

Biennial: A plant that grows vegetatively one year; flowers, fruits, and seeds the next; and then dies.

Border: A garden bed that is designed to edge or frame something, often backed by a wall, hedge, or fence.

Bract: A colorful, leaflike structure that appears below a flower, such as the showy part of a dogwood or poinsettia "flower."

Brushwood: Twigs cut in late winter to use for staking plants. Birch twigs are ideal.

Clump: Stems or underground shoots with several vegetative buds.

Cottage garden: Garden based on an English style of gardening in which many plants are placed in a dense and seemingly random fashion.

Cross-pollinate: When a flower of one plant is fertilized by the pollen from a flower of another plant.

Crown: The part of a plant where the roots are attached to the shoots.

Cultivation: To work the soil by digging, forking, hoeing, or using a mechanical device.

Cutting garden: A bed for growing flowers to harvest.

Deadheading: The removal of spent flowers to tidy up a plant and force it to put its energy into producing more flowers instead of seeds.

Division: A method of propagation in which the crown of a plant is divided into two or more pieces.

Double-flowered: A flower with more than the usual number of petals.

Ephemeral: A plant that has a very short growth cycle.

Eye: A ring of a deeper or paler color around the center of the flower; for example, many garden phlox and some dianthus have eye rings.

Floret: A small flower that makes up part of a large flower head.

Flower head: A flower composed of many small flowers.

Flush: Abundant new growth produced after dormancy or being cut back.

Foundation plant: A plant placed next to a building to hide the foundation and soften the hard architectural lines.

Genus: A group of closely related species.

Ground cover: Plants that are used to cover bare ground; they usually spread to form dense colonies that choke out weeds.

Humus: Dark, fine-textured material that results from organic material reaching an advanced stage of decay.

Hybrid: A plant that results from cross-pollination of genetically dissimilar plants.

Inflorescence: The flowering part of a plant.

Interplant: To place plants between other plants to extend seasonal interest—such as planting spring bulbs among plants like hosta that develop later.

Island bed: A flower bed that you can walk around.

Leaf compost: Organic matter made from leaves that have been allowed to decay. Also called leaf mold.

Limestone: A soil amendment containing calcium; it slowly raises the pH of a soil so it is more alkaline (basic). Dolomitic limestone is the safest form to use. If soil tests indicate adequate magnesium, then calcitic limestone is the safest form to use.

Meadow gardening: Growing plants in an open area resembling an uncultivated field. Undesirable species are cut back or eliminated.

Mulch: A layer of organic or inorganic material placed around plants to hold in moisture and reduce weeds.

Peat moss: A usually weed-free form of organic matter created by the partial decomposition of sphagnum moss. It increases soil acidity.

Pinching: Snipping out (or using fingernails to literally pinch out) the growing point of a plant to promote fullness and bushiness.

Powdery mildew: A disease that coats the upper surface of leaves and flowers with a pale gray or white dustlike growth.

Propagate: To create new plants.

Raised bed: A bed that is higher than the surrounding area, often contained within a low retaining wall composed of rocks, bricks, logs, or boards.

Recurrent bloom (repeat blooming): Blooming after the main flush of flowers has passed.

Semidouble: A flower with two or three rows of petals.

Semiwoody: A perennial that has shrublike stems.

Sepal: The usually green part of many flowers that encloses the petals and reproductive organs.

Single-flowered: A flower with a single row of petals.

Species: A group of plants within a genus that are more or less identical.

Spike: A long, usually unbranched flower stem.

Stamen: The male reproductive organ in a flower where pollen is produced.

Stem cuttings: Pieces of shoots cut from a plant to create new plants.

Tepal: Parts of a flower that are not petals or sepals, but look like them; for example, the showy parts of tulip flowers are tepals.

Transplant: To dig up and relocate a plant.

True to variety: A plant whose seedling offspring are identical in appearance to the parent plant.

Underplant: To plant flowers or bulbs beneath the canopy of a larger plant to add color to the garden without taking up additional space.

Variegated leaves: Leaves that are patterned in a different color.

Variety: A subdivision of a species; commonly used in place of the horticultural term *cultivar,* which is a cultivated variety.

Well-drained soil: Soil that drains quickly, even after heavy rain.

Wet feet: A term for a plant that is sitting in waterlogged soil.

Whorl: A circle of three or more leaves or flowers around a plant stem.

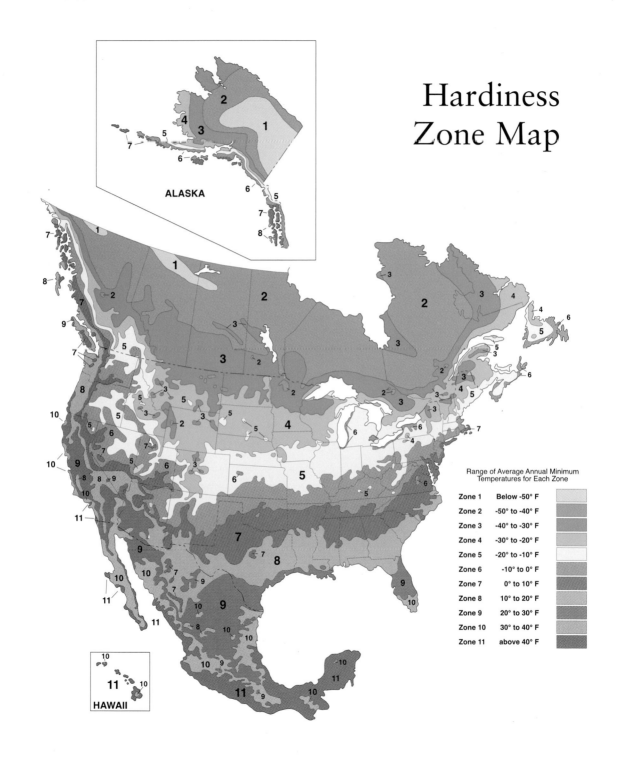

Hardiness Zone Map

ALASKA

HAWAII

Range of Average Annual Minimum
Temperatures for Each Zone

Zone 1	Below -50° F	
Zone 2	-50° to -40° F	
Zone 3	-40° to -30° F	
Zone 4	-30° to -20° F	
Zone 5	-20° to -10° F	
Zone 6	-10° to 0° F	
Zone 7	0° to 10° F	
Zone 8	10° to 20° F	
Zone 9	20° to 30° F	
Zone 10	30° to 40° F	
Zone 11	above 40° F	

PHOTOGRAPHY & ILLUSTRATION CREDITS

Derek Fell
Front cover, back cover, title page,
3, 12, 14, 16, 20, 24, 26, 36, 38,
42, 46, 48, 56, 68, 72, 74, 76, 80,
84, 88, 90, 92, 98, 102, 106, 110,
116

Bill Johnson
40, 58, 62, 108.

Jerry Pavia
28, 44, 70, 78, 82, 86, 94, 96.

Richard Shiell
10, 18, 30, 32, 54, 60, 66, 112,
114

Joseph Strauch, Jr
34, 50, 52, 64, 104

Steven Swinburn
22, 100

Illustrator: Anna Dewdney

INDEX

Storey Communications, Inc.
Pownal, Vermont

President: M. John Storey
Executive Vice President: Martha M. Storey
Chief Operating Officer: Dan Reynolds
Director of Custom Publishing: Deirdre Lynch
Project Manager: Barbara Weiland
Author: Michael Dodge
Book Design: Betty Kodela
Design Assistance: Erin Lincourt, Jen Rork
Horticultural Review: Charles W. G. Smith